CAMPAIGN 424

GULF WAR 1990–91

Saddam's Iraq Faces Operation *Desert Storm*

STEVEN J. ZALOGA ILLUSTRATED BY ROBERT McSWEENEY

OSPREY PUBLISHING
Bloomsbury Publishing Plc
Kemp House, Chawley Park, Cumnor Hill, Oxford OX2 9PH, UK
Bloomsbury Publishing Ireland Limited,
29 Earlsfort Terrace, Dublin 2, D02 AY28, Ireland
Bloomsbury Publishing Inc.
1359 Broadway, 12th Floor, New York, NY 10018, USA
E-mail: info@ospreypublishing.com
www.ospreypublishing.com

OSPREY is a trademark of Osprey Publishing Ltd

First published in Great Britain in 2026

© Osprey Publishing Ltd, 2026

All rights reserved. No part of this publication may be: i) reproduced or transmitted in any form, electronic or mechanical, including photocopying, recording or by means of any information storage or retrieval system without prior permission in writing from the publishers; or ii) used or reproduced in any way for the training, development or operation of artificial intelligence (AI) technologies, including generative AI technologies. The rights holders expressly reserve this publication from the text and data mining exception as per Article 4(3) of the Digital Single Market Directive (EU) 2019/790.

A catalog record for this book is available from the British Library.

ISBN: PB 9781472868909; eBook 9781472868916; ePDF 9781472868886; XML 9781472868893

26 27 28 29 30 10 9 8 7 6 5 4 3 2 1

Maps by Bounford.com
3D BEVs by Paul Kime
Index by Fionbar Lyons
Typeset by Lumina Datamatics Ltd
Printed by Repro India Ltd

Author's note

The author would like to thank Stephen (Cookie) Sewell and Matt Reeves for their help with Iraqi unit identifications.

Transliterations of geographic names from the Arabic vary from source to source, and the versions used here are those common in US Department of Defense accounts.

Unless otherwise noted, all photos used in this book are from US Department of Defense organizations and DoD photos archived by other government organizations such as NARA.

Glossary

ACR	US armored cavalry regiment
AFB	air force base
AFV	armored fighting vehicle
CENTCOM	US Central Command
CFV	Cavalry Fighting Vehicle
CIA	US Central Intelligence Agency
Daguet	French operation in 1991 Gulf War
Desert Shield	US buildup operation in Saudi Arabia in 1990
Desert Storm	US combat operation in 1991 Gulf War
DIA	US Defense Intelligence Agency
GCC	Gulf Cooperation Council
GMID	Iraqi General Military Intelligence Directorate
Granby	British operation in 1991 Gulf War
IFV	infantry fighting vehicle
JCS	US Joint Chiefs of Staff
JFC	Joint Forces Command
JSTARS	E-8A Joint Surveillance Target Attack Radar System
KTO	Kuwait Theater of Operations
Mech	Mechanized
MEF	Marine Expeditionary Force
MLRS	Multiple Launch Rocket System
MODA	Saudi Ministry of Defense and Aviation
OP	Observation Post
RGFC	Iraqi Republican Guard Forces Command
RSLF	Royal Saudi Land Forces
SANG	Saudi Arabia National Guard
SPH	self-propelled howitzer
TEL	transporter-erector-launcher (vehicle for ballistic missile system)
USMC	United States Marine Corps

Osprey Publishing supports the Woodland Trust, the UK's leading woodland conservation charity.

To find out more about our authors and books visit www.ospreypublishing.com. Here you will find extracts, author interviews, details of forthcoming events and the option to sign up for our newsletter.

For product safety related questions contact productsafety@bloomsbury.com

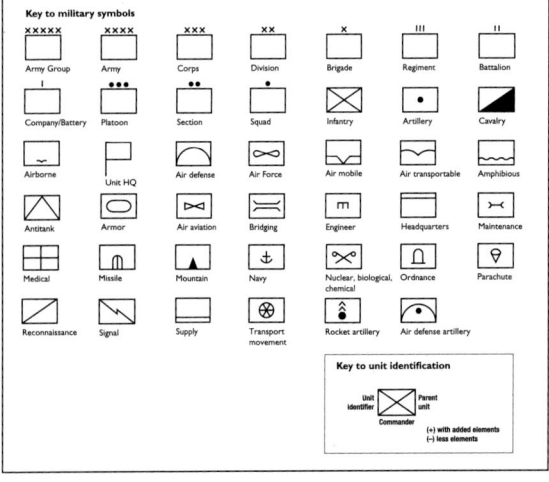

Front cover main illustration: Apache attack at the Battle of Rumaylah, March 2, 1991. (Robert McSweeney)
Title page photograph: Jubilation as Saudi and Kuwaiti units liberate Kuwait City on February 26, 1991.

CONTENTS

INTRODUCTION	4
CHRONOLOGY	6
OPPOSING COMMANDERS	8
Iraq . Coalition	
OPPOSING FORCES	11
Iraq . Coalition . Orders of battle	
OPPOSING PLANS	32
Iraq . Coalition	
THE CAMPAIGN	37

Casus belli: The invasion of Kuwait . The air campaign . Missile war . Iraqi raid at Khafji . The ground campaign begins: Joint Forces Command and the I MEF . The "Great Wheel" begins: XVIII Airborne Corps . The Great Wheel's heavy metal: VII Corps . The withdrawal order . Battles with the Republican Guard . The liberation of Kuwait City . Endgame

THE CAMPAIGN IN RETROSPECT	90
THE BATTLEFIELD TODAY	92
FURTHER READING	93
INDEX	95

INTRODUCTION

In 1980, Iraq invaded neighboring Iran, precipitating a bitter eight-year war. By the end of the 1980s, Iraq was bankrupt, having amassed enormous debts to conduct the war. In 1990, Iraqi dictator Saddam Hussein began eyeing Iraq's southern neighbor, the oil-rich country of Kuwait. Iraq had long claimed that Kuwait rightly was part of greater Iraq, often called its "19th Province." For Saddam, the pillage of Kuwait was a quick fix for Iraq's crippling economic problems.

Iraq began to broadcast hostile propaganda in July 1990 about Kuwait's alleged perfidious behavior as it ramped up for war. On July 21, 1990, Iraq began the first steps towards military invasion, moving one of its Republican Guard Forces Command (RGFC) armored divisions to the northern Kuwait border. On August 1, 1990, the US Central Command (CENTCOM) went to WATCHCON I, warning that Iraq would invade Kuwait.

Iraq's August 1990 invasion of Kuwait was a speedy military victory pitting one of the largest Arab armies against one of the smallest. Kuwait fell in a few days. Saddam's aggression infuriated neighboring Saudi Arabia, placing the large Iraqi Army within striking distance of Riyadh. An American intelligence assessment warned that Iraq could overrun and secure Kuwait in four days, at which time it could invade Saudi Arabia and reach the port and oil facilities of al-Jubayl in Saudi Arabia in five days.

Iraq's aggrandizement upset the balance of military power in the Gulf region. This was of worldwide concern due to international dependence on oil supplies from Saudi Arabia and the other countries of the Gulf Cooperation Council (GCC). The Saudi monarchy began negotiations with the United States, Britain, and France to create a coalition to oust Iraq from Kuwait. On August 4, 1990, US President George H. W. Bush and the US National Security Council decided to begin preparations for a military response. On August 9, the United Nations Security Council, including the Soviet Union, passed Resolution 662 declaring the Iraqi annexation of Kuwait to be null and void. Eventually, more than 30 countries would join the Coalition, many indebted to Saudi Arabia for decades of economic support.

The United States, Britain, and France had long been troubled by Iraq's belligerence as well as Saddam's pursuit of weapons-of-mass-destruction. The end of the Cold War in Europe in 1991 following the dissolution of the Warsaw Pact freed up a large contingent of military forces in Germany that could be readily transported to the Gulf.

The Coalition decided to take a cautious approach to the campaign against Iraq. Iraq had built up a substantial army during its war with Iran. There was concern that it might still constitute a battle-hardened and experienced foe.

To weaken the Iraqi Army before the final ground campaign, in January 1991 the Coalition began a month-long air campaign, aimed at crippling the Iraqi forces in Kuwait. This book does not detail the air campaign since it has already been covered in an Osprey Air Campaign title.[1] Nor does it cover the associated naval operations in order to focus on the ground campaign.

Iraq had hoped that its large and expensive network of air defense missiles and guns would blunt the Coalition air attack. This network utterly failed against the far more sophisticated Coalition air forces. Saddam was unwilling to pit his air force against the Coalition. In one of the more bizarre incidents of the war, the Iraqi Air Force was ordered to seek refuge with its long-time foe in neighboring Iran. By the end of the air campaign, the Iraqi Army in Kuwait had been battered and demoralized.

The Iraqi response to the air campaign was a series of raids into Saudi Arabia in January 1991. The largest of these was the capture of the Saudi port city of Ras al-Khafji. The battle for Khafji backfired on Iraq. Instead of displaying its military prowess, the inept conduct of the Khafji assault convinced Coalition leaders that Iraq was a paper tiger, albeit a well-armed one.

One of the few weapons available to Iraq that could circumvent the Coalition was its arsenal of modified Scud missiles. These were launched against Coalition bases in Saudi Arabia. Saddam also hoped that he might undermine the Coalition with missile attacks against Israel, hoping to exploit the anti-Israeli sentiment of the Muslim coalition members. This scheme failed and the United States deployed Patriot missile batteries to defend Israel against the Scud attacks.

G-Day, the start of the ground campaign, began on February 24, 1991. The Joint Forces Command (JFC) under Saudi direction attacked across Kuwait's southern border, aiming for Kuwait City. This force, containing the US I Marine Expeditionary Force along with the Saudi and other Arab units, faced the bulk of Iraqi defenses in the Kuwait Theater of Operations (KTO). The strongest Coalition force, the VII Corps, contained most of the US Army heavy maneuver divisions as well as the British 1st Armoured Division. With JFC tying down the Iraqi Army in Kuwait, the XVIII Airborne Corps and VII Corps began a bold maneuver through the desert west of Kuwait. The "Great Wheel" aimed to trap and destroy the elite Republican Guard Command in northern Iraq.

The Iraqi Army collapsed. The ground campaign was over in 100 hours in one of the most humiliating defeats in recent military history. Although it was a resounding military victory for the Coalition, the final political consequences were controversial. The defeat failed to unseat Saddam, and conflict would resume a decade later.

---

1   Richard P. Hallion, Desert Storm *1991: The most shattering air campaign in history*, Air Campaign Series, Osprey Publishing: Oxford (2022)

CHRONOLOGY

1990

August 2	Iraq invades Kuwait
August 6	Saudi Arabia requests assistance from United States; UN authorizes sanctions against Iraq
August 7	President George H. W. Bush orders start of Operation *Desert Shield*
August 7	C-Day: a brigade of the 82nd Airborne Division dispatched to al-Jubayl, Saudi Arabia
August 12	First ships carrying US troops arrive in Saudi Arabia
September	RGFC units pull out of Kuwait to defensive positions along the northern border
October 11	Senior US leaders hold a meeting and decide a larger force commitment will be needed
October 31	Size of final US force package for KTO decided at White House
November 8	President Bush announces plans to add a further 200,000 US troops to *Desert Shield*
November 8	US Army's VII Corps ordered to deploy to KTO
November 29	US Security Council Resolution 678 authorizes "all necessary means" to evict Iraq from Kuwait

1991

January 12	US Congress authorizes use of force in Kuwait
January 15	UN deadline for Iraqi withdrawal occurs
January 15	Bush signs National Security Directive 54 authorizing military action in KTO
January 17	Coalition air campaign starts at 0200hrs (Gulf time)
January 17	Iraq begins first Luna-M/FROG-7 rocket attacks against Saudi Arabia
January 18	Iraq begins first Scud missile attacks against Israel
January 20	Iraq begins first Scud attacks against Saudi Arabia
January 25	Iraqi Air Force stages sole air attack of the campaign against Saudi oil terminal at Ras Tanura
January 29	Iraqi Army launches spoiling attack into Ras al-Khafji
January 30	Saudi Arabia National Guard (SANG) launches attacks to retake Khafji
February 1	SANG recaptures Khafji

February 20	Coalition forces begin preparatory actions along Saddam Line
February 24	G-Day: ground campaign begins
February 25	Iraq launches armored counter-attack against I Marine Expeditionary Force (I MEF)
February 25	Saddam orders withdrawal of Iraqi Army from Kuwait in late afternoon
February 26	I MEF reaches outskirts of Kuwait International Airport
February 26	Battle of 73 Easting against RGFC
February 27	Battle of Medina Ridge against RGFC
February 27	I MEF in control of Kuwait International Airport, reaches Kuwait City outskirts
February 28	Ground campaign ends with unilateral ceasefire at 0800hrs
March 2	Battle of the Hammar Causeway
March 3	Iraq accepts ceasefire at meeting at Safwan airbase
March 10	US forces begin withdrawing from Kuwait
April 11	UN Security Council formally concludes the war

OPPOSING COMMANDERS

IRAQ

Saddam Hussein was the dominant military leader at both the strategic and operational level. He was born to a Sunni Arab family near Tikrit in 1937 and joined the Baath Party at age 20 in 1957. The Baath Party espoused a pan-Arabist and socialist philosophy. He rose steadily in the party and played an important role in the coup in July 1968 that brought the Baath Party to power. Saddam was appointed vice president of Iraq by Ahmed Hassan al-Bakr, the leader of the coup. Saddam consolidated political power within the Iraqi Baath movement through the 1970s, gradually taking over power, and finally becoming the de facto dictator of Iraq following al-Bakr's resignation in 1979. He led the Iraqi armed forces during the Second Iraqi–Kurdish War in 1974–75. The Baath Party became increasingly totalitarian under Saddam, creating a police state patterned on communist regimes. The state was run by the Sunni minority and dominated the Shia Arab majority and other groups such as the Kurds in the north. Saddam favored Sunnis from his ancestral Tikrit region for senior leadership positions.

Saddam Hussein, chairman of the Revolutionary Command Council and dictator of Iraq.

Saddam was the primary instigator behind the 1980–88 war with Iran. He perceived the revolutionary Shia theocratic leadership of Iran as a threat to the Arab world, proclaiming Iraq as the bulwark of Arab power against the traditional Persian foe. After early Iraqi victories, the conflict bogged down into a costly war of attrition. Saddam oversaw a major modernization of the Iraqi armed forces with new weaponry from the Soviet Union, Europe, and China, partly funded from sympathetic Arab states. With both sides exhausted, the war ended with no gains for either side. The Iran–Iraq War left Iraq saddled with substantial international debt in excess of US$10 billion.

By 1989, Saddam began to see the absorption of Kuwait by Iraq as a solution to Iraq's debt problem, as well as an additional source of long-term wealth due to its extensive oil fields. Rather than demobilize after the failed Iran–Iraq War, the Iraqi Army began combined-arms training in the summer of 1989, preparing for another war. In the summer of 1989, Saddam tasked Lt. Gen. Aayad Futayyih Khalifa al-Rawi, the chief of staff of the Iraqi RGFC, to begin planning for the invasion of Kuwait. It is worth noting that the chief of staff of the regular Iraqi Army, Gen. Nizar al-Khazraji, was not a part of this planning process. The invasion was prepared by a very small number of senior RGFC commanders along with Saddam and key Baath leaders such as foreign minister Tariq Azziz.

Saddam had a blinkered world view, having spent little time outside of Iraq. His military ideas were dominated by his romantic notion that the inherent warrior spirit of the Iraqi soldier, proven through history, would make modern military technology irrelevant. One of his senior commanders, Gen. Ra'ad al-Hamdani, later remarked that Saddam "tended to confuse reality with what he wished to be true." Senior Iraqi commanders were chosen for their loyalty to Saddam rather than military skills. Saddam's dominant role over Iraq and his shortcomings as a military leader doomed the Iraqi Army in the 1991 war.

Lt. Gen. Sultan Ahmed Hashim al-Tai, Iraqi Army chief of staff and later Minister of Defense, and behind him, Lt. Gen. Salah Aboud Mahmoud, the 3 Corps commander, at the ceasefire talks in Safwan at the end of the Gulf War.

COALITION

United States

At the time of the 1990 war, the US Secretary of Defense was Dick Cheney, a career politician selected for the role by President George H. W. Bush. Cheney selected Gen. Colin Powell as the head of the US Joint Chiefs of Staff in 1989. Powell had served as a young army officer during the Vietnam War and had developed a strong distaste for the style of leadership during the conflict, with the then-Secretary of Defense, Robert McNamara, micromanaging the armed services. His own strategic vision was dubbed the Powell Doctrine: avoid American military intervention unless it involved key American national security interests, employ overwhelming force, and ensure widespread public support. Powell and Cheney dominated American strategic decision-making during the 1991 Gulf War.

By the early 1990s, the US armed forces were shifting to a regional command structure to manage military affairs around the globe. The Middle East was under the purview of CENTCOM, commanded since 1988 by **Gen. Norman Schwarzkopf, Jr**. He had served as an advisor to the army of Vietnam during the Vietnam War and subsequently as an army infantry battalion commander. He was decorated with three Silver Stars as well as two Purple Hearts during the war and had been a senior army leader during the invasion of Grenada in 1983. Like many army veterans

The most influential US military leaders during Operation *Desert Storm* were Secretary of Defense Dick Cheney, chairman of the Joint Chiefs of Staff Gen. Colin Powell, and head of CENTCOM, Gen. Norman Schwarzkopf.

of the Vietnam War, he was deeply disenchanted with national strategic leadership during the conflict and shared many of Powell's reservations about casually committing the US armed forces in any future war.

CENTCOM included subordinate commands for the armed services: ARCENT was the army element, comprised of the US Third Army under Lt. Gen. John Yeosock; CENTAF was the US Ninth Air Force under Lt. Gen. Charles Horner; NAVCENT was the US Seventh Fleet under Vice Adm. Stanley Arthur; and MARCENT was the I Marine Expeditionary Force under Lt. Gen. Walter Boomer.

Saudi Arabia

Saudi Arabia played the central role in assembling a large coalition of Arab and Muslim nations to support the coalition against Iraq. These units were organized under the JFC. King Fahd appointed **His Royal Highness Lt. Gen. Khalid bin Sultan al-Saud** to command the JFC in October 1990. Prince Khalid received his military education at the UK's Royal Military Academy at Sandhurst, the US Army's Command and General Staff College at Fort Leavenworth, and the US Air War College at Maxwell Air Force Base. Prior to the Gulf War, he was most closely associated with the formation of the first Saudi ballistic missile units, as well as the growth and expansion of the Saudi air defense missile forces. His subordinate commanders were Maj. Gen. Sulaiman al-Wuhayyib leading JFC-North and Maj. Gen. Sultan Adi al-Mutairi with JFC-East. War planning was managed by the Ministry of Defense and Aviation J3 (Operations) that established a special Joint Forces/Theater of Operations J5 office reporting to Prince Khalid.

United Kingdom

The British Forces Middle East (BFME) was led by **Lt. Gen. Sir Peter de la Billière**. His military career was most closely associated with the SAS (Special Air Service), first serving during the Malayan Emergency and subsequently in Oman, where he was awarded the Military Cross in 1959. In 1964–66, he served in Borneo, where he was awarded a bar to his Military Cross. He was in command of the SAS Group at the time of their storming of the Iranian Embassy in 1980. Although ready for retirement in 1990, he was selected to lead the British forces in Operation *Granby* due to his past experiences in the region and fluency in Arabic. The UK 1st Armoured Division was led by Maj. Gen. Rupert Smith.

The head of the JFC was Saudi Prince Lt. Gen. Khalid bin Sultan al-Saud.

France

The French contingent for Operation *Daguet* was commanded by **Général d'armée Michel Roquejeoffre**. He was most closely associated with the French parachute forces, first serving in the Algerian war in the 1950s, and subsequently in several overseas actions including Lebanon and Chad. He had commanded the 7e Division Blindée since 1987 and led the Rapid Action Force (FAR: Force d'action rapide) prior to his appointment to command Operation *Daguet*.

OPPOSING FORCES

IRAQ

The Iraqi Army in 1991 numbered 67 divisions, including 12 RGFC divisions. Of these, more than 45 were committed to the fighting in the KTO in February 1991. Although large and reasonably well armed, in reality it was a hollow force. The Iraqi ground forces included three major components: the army, the People's Army, and the Republican Guard Forces. As the name implies, the army was the main element of the ground forces and by far its largest component. The People's Army was a militia force and not extensively used in the 1990–91 war. The Republican Guard Forces were the praetorian guard of the Baath Party.

Tactical initiative in Iraqi Army operations was handicapped by the centralized control of Saddam Hussein's regime. Decision-making was centralized in Baghdad, and the paranoia instilled by the Baathist police state encouraged tactical commanders to strictly follow orders and discouraged personal initiative or flexibility. Many Iraqi Army commanders were shot for their failures during the Iran–Iraq War under Saddam's orders. While this type of authoritarian command-and-control proved adequate against the slow-moving and inept Iranian army in the 1980s war, such rigidity was poorly suited to a fast-moving war of maneuver that the Iraqi Army confronted in 1991.

Iraqi Army organization through the 1960s was patterned on the British General Staff model, but gradually changed in the late 1970s with an influx of Soviet weapons and advisors. In January 1990, there were 8,174 Soviet military advisers and specialists in Iraq, including 92 generals and 5,507 officers. They were all recalled by Moscow following the invasion of Kuwait due to Mikhail Gorbachev's disapproval of Saddam's 1990 war.

The Iraqi regular army was organized in the usual fashion with infantry, mechanized, and armored divisions. The infantry divisions were based around three infantry brigades plus a single tank regiment. The Iraqi tank units are variously identified as battalions or regiments but were closer to US battalions in size. Iraqi divisions varied in strength; there were usually about 8,000 men in a well-equipped infantry division, significantly smaller than contemporary NATO divisions. The infantry divisions were mediocre at best, with the better troops and commanders reserved for the armored and mechanized divisions.

Deployment of the Iraqi Army, February 23, 1991

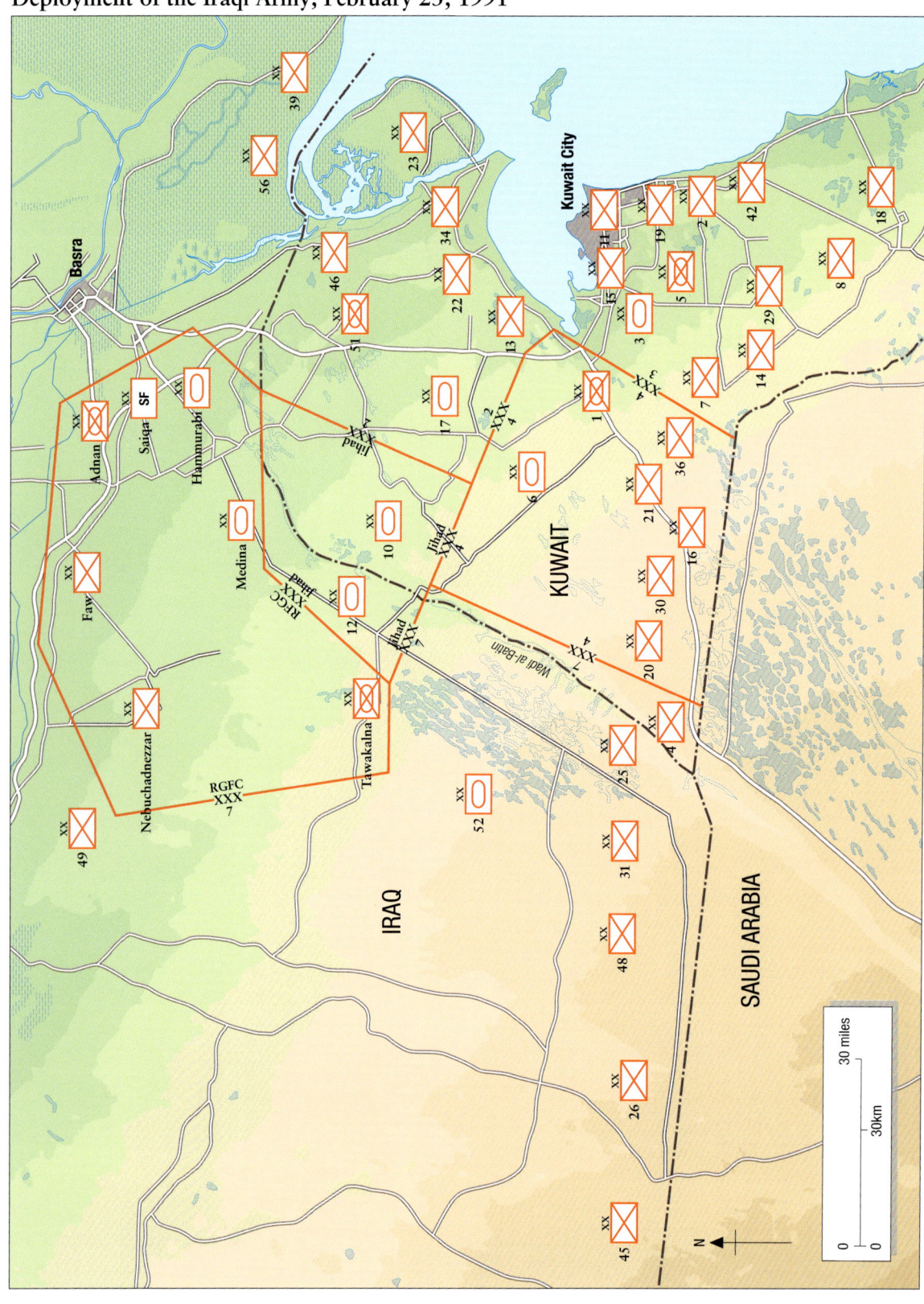

Iraq attempted to upgrade some of their older tank types with technical innovations. The "al-Fao" tank was a T-55 fitted with an array of non-explosive reactive armor boxes around the hull and turret to better protect it against antitank missiles. This upgrade was better known as the Enigma tank by Coalition forces.

Iraqi infantry divisions in 1991 invariably relied on defensive strongpoints with an ample defensive barrier in front consisting of minefields and other obstructions including fire trenches. The defensive width of Iraqi infantry divisions in 1991 depended on their location. Those along the eastern Kuwaiti border with Saudi Arabia had relatively narrow frontages about 10km in width. The frontages increased west of Wadi al-Batin with the divisions on the extreme left flank having frontages of 35km. Wadi al-Batin was the dry riverbed that formed the western border between Iraq and Kuwait.

Both the armored and mechanized divisions had a nominal organization of three maneuver brigades with the armored division having two tank and one mechanized infantry brigade, while the mechanized division had the ratio reversed with two mechanized infantry and one tank brigade. A tank brigade generally had three tank regiments and a mechanized infantry regiment, while a mechanized regiment reversed the ratio in favor of mechanized infantry regiments. The armored and mechanized divisions were the best element of the regular Iraqi Army, and some such as the 3rd Armored Division were favored with better equipment, including T-72 tanks and BMP-1 infantry vehicles.

The armored and mechanized divisions were generally deployed in the second echelon behind the infantry divisions. Their role was primarily to serve as a counter-attack force. Usually, each corps had a counter-attack force of two heavy maneuver divisions behind it for this mission. The weakest was the 7 Corps west of Kuwait, which had the new and inexperienced 52nd Armored Division spread out behind it. Many of these heavy maneuver forces had specific missions. For example, the Jihad Corps of the 10th and 12th Armored Divisions was positioned at the northern end of the Wadi al-Batin riverbed on Kuwait's western border specifically to counter-attack down either side of this natural terrain feature. The 51st Mechanized Division was deployed in northeastern Kuwait as a counter-airborne force since the Iraqi war plan predicted a Coalition airborne landing to seize the airbases north of Kuwait City.

The BMP-1 was the premium infantry fighting vehicle in the Iraqi Army, with preference going to the Republican Guard. Iraq obtained about 740 of these in 1981–86, of which about 290 came from Czechoslovakia and the rest from the Soviet Union.

The RGFC shifted from its original role of defense of the Baath government to a new role as the main strategic reserve of the ground forces. During the Iran–Iraq War, it was most often used as a counter-attack force. Its unit organization was similar to the regular army, but it was issued better equipment and its divisions were closer to official tables-of-organization than the regular army. So, RGFC divisions tended to have the Soviet/Warsaw Pact T-72M tank and BMP-1 infantry fighting vehicle, while regular army divisions tended to have the Chinese Type 69-II tanks and YW-531 or MT-LB armored personnel carriers.

Iraqi equipment in 1991 was very diverse due to problems purchasing equipment in the Iran–Iraq War, as well as war losses in 1980–88. Although much of the equipment was of Soviet origin, a Soviet arms embargo early in the war forced Iraq to go shopping elsewhere, with China becoming a significant supplier. The chart below is from a recently declassified CIA handbook covering arms exports for the period of 1981–86, during the peak of Iraqi weapons acquisition. Although it does not provide a complete inventory of the Iraqi arsenal, it does provide a glimpse of its variety.

Iraqi arms imports 1981–86

Tanks

Type 59	161	China
Type 69-II	2,000	China
T-55	1,049	Poland, USSR, other
T-62	151	USSR
T-72	945	USSR, Czechoslovakia

Light AFVs

EE-9 Cascavel	160	Brazil
EE-11 Urutu	104	Brazil
YW-531	1,221	China
AMX-10P	10	France
Type 6614	230	Italy
BTR-60PB	192	USSR
BMP-1	741	USSR, Czechoslovakia
BMD-1	118	USSR
MT-LB	255	USSR, Bulgaria

Antitank missiles

Milan	2,242	France
HOT	410	France

Multiple rocket launchers

122mm BM-21 Grad	90	USSR
122mm Type 81	58	China
122mm APR-40	34	Romania

Towed artillery

122mm Type 60	102	China
122mm D-30	104	USSR
130mm M-46	52	USSR
130mm M-46	400	Romania
130mm Type 59-1	254	China
130mm Type 59-1	196	North Korea
152mm Type 66	373	China
155mm GHN-45	200	Austria
155mm G5	54	South Africa

Self-propelled artillery

122mm Type 54	11	China
122mm 2S1	49	USSR
152mm 2S3	18	USSR
155mm GCT	76	France
155mm Palmaria	3	Italy

Source: *Handbook of Major Foreign Weapon Systems Exported to the Third World 1981–1986*, Directorate of Intelligence, CIA, November 1987; *Iraq: Major Weapon Deliveries and Their Impact on Force Capabilities*, Directorate of Intelligence, CIA, February 1987

The Iraqi tank force was built around the old Soviet T-55 tank and its Chinese equivalent, the Type 69-II. The Chinese Type 69-II was often called the T-55B in Iraqi service. These tanks were armed with 100mm guns that could not penetrate the frontal armor of any of the better Coalition tanks, such as the Abrams or Challenger. At the same time, their armor was vulnerable to most Coalition anti-armor weapons. Some Iraqi units received the better T-62 tank, but these were not especially common. Many of the older tanks were worn out from their use in the Iran–Iraq War. For example, the tank regiment of the 27th Infantry Division had 34 T-55 tanks but 17 of these were unserviceable and sent back to Iraq for repair, never to return. Other units were significantly below strength. For example, the 52nd Armored Brigade of the 52nd Armored Division had only half of its authorized 90 tanks.

The best Iraqi tank was the T-72, obtained from the Soviet Union, Czechoslovakia, and Poland. Some of these were the baseline T-72 Ural version, but some of the improved T-72M1 were obtained in the years immediately before the war from Poland. There was a scheme to locally manufacture the T-72M in Iraq based on Polish technical assistance, but this never came to fruition. The T-72 was the Soviet mobilization tank, intended for

During the Iran–Iraq War, Iraq purchased weapons from a wide range of suppliers. This is an EE-9 Cascavel armored car, purchased from the Brazilian Engesa firm, that served in the 10th "Nasr ibn Sayyar" Armored Division in the 1991 war. Iraq obtained 576 Cascavels and 104 EE-11 Urutus from Brazil during the buying binge in 1981–86.

China exported over 1,220 YW-531 armored transporters of various sub-types to Iraq in 1981–86, where they were locally called the BTR-63. This is a YW-701A command version near the al-Mutla police station, of which Iraq received at least 144, including the similar YW-750 ambulance version.

second echelon unit and not used by the premier Soviet tank units in East Germany that were equipped with the T-64 or T-80. The T-72 generally had inferior fire controls and armored protection than the comparable T-64 and T-80 variants. In addition, the Soviet Union did not sell Iraq its better 125mm tank ammunition.

The Iraqi Army had a very motley selection of armored infantry vehicles since budget priorities favored tank purchases. The most common were the Chinese YW-531 armored personnel carriers (APC). These were a simple "battle-taxi" similar to the US Army's M113 APC. The RGFC and the elite army armored divisions generally received the better Soviet BMP-1 infantry fighting vehicle that was armed with a 73mm low-pressure gun and a Malyutka (AT-3 Sagger) antitank missile.

Iraq had plentiful towed artillery, mainly Soviet designs or their Chinese copies. A small number of high-end types were obtained, notably the South African G5 developed by the controversial engineer Gerald Bull. He later worked for Iraq on their special weapons programs, including the extended-range Scud missiles and on long-range artillery projects. Acquisition of self-propelled artillery was very limited. Iraq attempted to develop its own self-propelled artillery and paraded prototypes at the 1988 Baghdad industrial exhibition. However, these did not reach series production. Multiple rocket launchers were purchased in modest numbers. The best type was the Brazilian Astros system, and Iraq tried to manufacture its own examples. As in the case of the indigenous self-propelled artillery, this program did not reach serial production by 1990. In terms of artillery fire control, Iraq did acquire some Soviet artillery locating radars for counter-battery fire, as well as a number of armored artillery command post vehicles. These were few in number and Iraqi fire control was markedly inferior to that of the Coalition.

The Iraqi Army had a modest self-propelled artillery force, relying more heavily on towed weapons. This is a 2S1 Gvozdika 122mm self-propelled howitzer of an unidentified RGFC unit in a typical entrenchment. Iraq obtained about 50 of these before the war, of which at least seven came from Bulgaria and the rest from the Soviet Union.

The best Iraqi field gun was the G5 155mm gun imported from South Africa with an impressive 30km maximum range. Developed by the controversial engineer Gerald Bull, Iraq received 54 of these in 1986. This captured example was brought back to the US by the 24th Infantry Division (Mech) after the war. (Author)

The US Army found that the Iraqi artillery fired very sporadically against pre-registered targets; artillery fire was seldom adjusted during the course of the fighting. Although front-line infantry divisions were starved of food and other supplies, Iraqi artillery units tended to have very ample inventories of artillery ammunition that had been moved into Kuwait in the months before the start of the ground campaign.

Iraqi artillery seldom proved capable of conducting prolonged or accurate counter-battery fire, because US artillery batteries would engage Iraqi artillery as soon as they fired. A typical example was the 48th Infantry Division, which had 100 guns before the start of the air campaign, 90 guns before the start of the ground campaign, and no functional guns by the end of February 24 after the ground campaign began due to devastating Coalition counter-battery fire.

The Iraqi Army's weakest branch was air defense, particularly evident in light of the Coalition's extensive use of air power. The Iraqi Army did not face a serious air threat from Iran in the 1980s and Iraqi air defense tended to be perfunctory and not very modern. The maneuver divisions had three air defense battalions with a mixture of self-propelled, towed, and missile battalions. The self-propelled battalions nominally had nine ZSU-23-4 Shilka self-propelled, radar-directed 23mm guns, but a shortage of these led to the substitution of towed weapons. Towed antiaircraft battalions had a mixture of 14.5mm heavy machine guns, ZU-23 automatic cannon, Chinese/Soviet 37mm guns, or radar-directed 57mm S-60 guns. The missile battalions had nine Strela-1 (SA-9 Gaskin) armed with four infrared guided missiles on a BRDM-2 wheeled AFV. Iraqi infantry divisions received mainly towed antiaircraft guns. The Iraqi Army had numerous man-portable air-defense (MANPAD) missiles, including the outdated Strela-2M (SA-7 Grail) and some of the newer Strela-3 (SA-14) and Igla (SA-16). The Republican Guard had better quality equipment, including about a dozen Strela-10 (SA-13 Gopher), a more modern replacement for the Strela-1/SA-9. Long-range air defense systems such as the Kvadrat (SA-6 Gainful) were not used in their intended role for tactical defense but became part of the strategic air defense network in Iraq. The Iraqi radars used for air defense were limited in number and were vulnerable to Coalition electronic warfare tactics.

A ZSU-23-4 Shilka radar-directed quadruple 23mm antiaircraft gun system of 96th Air Defense Regiment, 1st "Abu Ubayda ibn al-Jarrah" Mechanized Division captured by the I MEF on the road leading to the Euphrates River valley.

The Iraqi Army's aviation branch split off from the air force in 1980. This consisted mainly of transport and utility helicopters; attack helicopters such as the Mi-24 were part of the air force. Helicopters were extensively used in the 1990 Kuwait invasion, including a bold heliborne air assault operation against Kuwait City. The aviation branch did not play a significant role in the 1991 ground campaign since their bases were attacked during the air campaign.

Ballistic missiles

Iraq placed considerable importance on its arsenal of ballistic missiles due to the shortcomings of its air force. Iraq acquired an R-17E Elbrus (Scud B) brigade in 1973, subsequently designated as Brigade 224. This consisted of 14 9P117 TELs (transporter-erector-launchers) based on the MAZ-543 8x8 all-terrain truck. When the Iran–Iraq War stalemated in 1983, Brigade 224 was ordered to attack Iranian cities along the frontier. The Iranians subsequently obtained Scud missiles from Libya and used them to attack Iraqi cities, including Baghdad. Since the Iraqi Scuds could not reach Tehran, Saddam ordered the start of the Project Mustafa/Project 144 to extend the range. The modified missile was dubbed the al-Husayn and they were used during the second "War of the Cities" starting on February 29, 1988. The al-Husayn had a range of 650km versus the Scud B's range of 300km. This was accomplished by lengthening the fuel cells to increase the fuel capacity by 990kg as well as reducing the warhead from 990kg to 650kg. At least ten TELs and one training launcher were still in service in 1991. Iraq tried to purchase more missiles and TELs from the Soviet Union but was informed that it was no longer in production and that there were no spare missiles for sale.

Iraq tried to expand its ballistic missile force before the war by building these al-Waleed mobile launchers based on a Scania 112H tractor truck towing a new erector-launcher trailer for the al-Husayn missile, as seen here during the 1989 Baghdad military industry show. Four of these served with Brigade 223 in the 1991 war.

Besides work on improved missiles, Iraqi engineers expanded the size of the missile force by building new launchers. Two types of mobile launchers were designed, the al-Waleed semi-trailer launcher and the simpler al-Nida. Six al-Waleed launchers were completed prior to the Gulf War, four equipping the new Brigade 223. A simple type of fixed launch erector was also designed, and 56 of these static launchers were under construction at airbases in the western Iraq desert, aimed at Israel. About two dozen had been completed by the end of 1990.

Besides the Scud brigades, the Iraqi Missile Corps also deployed Brigade 225 armed with 36 Luna-M (FROG-7) unguided ballistic rocket launchers and the Brigade 226 equipped with 24 Astros multiple rocket launchers obtained from Brazil.

The intelligence dimension

The Iraqi armed forces had relatively good intelligence capabilities from a regional perspective, though an order of magnitude poorer than the Coalition. The Iraqi effort was managed by the General Military Intelligence Directorate (GMID). The Iraqi capability to employ its intelligence collection in planning the conduct of the war was constrained by Saddam's personal control in most major decision-making, and his distortion of information due to his own misconceptions. For example, the Iraqi armed forces began to pick up hints of the presence of a major Coalition presence in the deserts west of Kuwait in February 1991, yet Saddam remained unwilling to consider that this force concentration might be the fulcrum of the Coalition ground campaign.

The Iraqi armed forces had a large and sophisticated intelligence collection system that one US report labeled as "the most sophisticated threat to face the US outside of the Soviet Union." For example, the Iraqi Air Force had MiG-21, MiG-25, and Mirage F-1EQ aircraft with imagery pods and side-looking radar. These flew missions daily along the frontier up until the start of the Coalition air campaign on January 17, 1991. There was also a comprehensive system of signals intelligence stations for monitoring radio networks. However, this was hampered by a severe shortage of English-language linguists. The Iraqis operated an extensive network of spies who infiltrated into Saudi Arabia under the guise of Kuwait refugees. The Coalition forces were aware of the Iraqi intelligence network and went to considerable effort to blind the Iraqi Army both by technical means as well as deception efforts.

COALITION

The multinational Coalition included forces from more than 30 countries. Many of these were small detachments sent to show solidarity with Saudi Arabia and took little part in the fighting. Some countries, such as Pakistan and Syria, sent sizeable forces that refrained from taking an active role in actual combat and so are not detailed here. The chart below gives a rough comparison of the major contributors. It should be noted that the units such as battalion and squadron refer to the size of typical US units; British and French regiments were close in size to the US battalions and so are listed as such here for comparison purposes.

Coalition contributions to the Kuwait campaign

	USA	UK	France	Egypt	Saudi	Kuwait
Tank battalions	34	3	1	9	6	2
Cavalry squadrons	14	1	2	2	4	
Infantry battalions	61	6	4	9	16	8
Helicopter battalions	21	4	2		1	1
Artillery battalions	59	5	1	14	8	3

United States

US Army and Marine units were the most numerous and significant element of the Coalition ground forces. The US Army had undergone a considerable renaissance since the end of the Vietnam War, converting from a conscript army to a professional force. A new generation of officers who had served in Vietnam, such as Powell and Schwarzkopf, had instituted broad reforms. New doctrines such as Air-Land Battle had reinvigorated army tactical thought. Innovations like the National Training Center had led to much more realistic training, with a focus on high-intensity, mechanized combat. A new generation of weapons had been introduced, including the M1 Abrams tank, Bradley fighting vehicle, and MLRS (Multiple Launch Rocket System).

Another important change was initiated by the 1979 hostage crisis when the new Iranian theocratic regime took the US embassy staff in Tehran hostage. A disastrous attempt to rescue the hostages highlighted the unpreparedness of the US armed forces for dealing with crises in the Middle East. This led to efforts to field a Rapid Deployment Force (RDF) oriented towards this mission. Although no formal RDF was created, many aspects of the concept were adopted, including CENTCOM to manage military affairs in the region. By the end of the Iran–Iraq War in 1988, CENTCOM became concerned about potential future conflicts in the region, and in July 1990 staged Internal Look 90, a command post exercise to examine various operational and logistical problems should war break out between Iraq and

Riflemen of the 3rd Platoon, Company A, 1st Battalion, 327th Infantry Regiment, 101st Airborne Division (Air Assault) following the conclusion of the fighting in the Euphrates River valley in March 1991. They are wearing the "chocolate-chip" battledress uniform so familiar during Operation *Desert Storm*.

Kuwait. Following King Fahd's decision to allow US forces to deploy on Saudi soil, CENTCOM established a forward headquarters in the basement of the Saudi Ministry of Defense and Aviation (MODA) building in Riyadh.

The US Marine Corps (USMC) saw the rapid deployment role as its central mission in the post-Vietnam era. Elements of the army, especially the two airborne divisions, also became oriented towards this mission. A Maritime Prepositioning Force (MPF) was created to provide enough equipment to sustain a Marine Corps Air-Ground Task Force for up to 30 days. The MPF forward deployed heavy equipment such as tanks on ships that would be difficult to move quickly by air.

The US buildup in the Gulf, codenamed Operation *Desert Shield*, started on C-Day, August 7, 1990, with the dispatch of a brigade of the 82nd Airborne Division at the Saudi port of al-Jubayl. By mid-October, the force had been expanded to include the rest of the 82nd Airborne Division as well as the 101st Airborne Division, 24th Infantry Division, 3rd Armored Cavalry Regiment, and the first of two Marine divisions.

The eventual US deployments for Operation *Desert Storm* in the Kuwait Theater of Operations (KTO) consisted of three main elements. The I Marine Expeditionary Force consisted of two USMC divisions, reinforced by an army armored brigade. The US Third Army oversaw two more corps. The larger of the two was VII Corps, which had been transferred from Germany. This included four US Army divisions, an armored cavalry regiment (ACR), and the UK 1st Armoured Division. The flanking force at the extreme western side of the Coalition was the XVIII Airborne Corps, including both US airborne divisions, a mechanized infantry division, an ACR, and the French Division Daguet.

Desert Shield and the subsequent *Desert Storm* campaigns required a substantial logistical effort. By early 1991, the US forces were being supplied with 62,000 ration packs, 9 million gallons of water, 24 million gallons of fuel, and 450 trailer loads of other supplies on a daily basis. By war's end, US operations had consumed 95,000 tons of ammunition and 1.7 billion gallons of fuel.

The US Army heavy maneuver divisions were organized into two or three brigades. The armored divisions' brigades typically included three to four battalion-sized task forces. These were usually combined-arms formations including tank companies, mechanized infantry companies, or cavalry squadrons. The mechanized infantry divisions had a similar organization, though the ratio of Abrams tank battalions and Bradley mechanized infantry battalions on paper was different, with only four tank battalions in the infantry divisions versus six in the armored divisions, but correspondingly more Bradley battalions. US heavy maneuver divisions in the KTO often use modified Tables-of-Organization & Equipment (TO&E), for example, in the composition of their divisional armored cavalry. The 1st Infantry Division, 24th Infantry Division, and 1st Cavalry Division retained their traditional names, but were in fact mechanized infantry formations.

Each of the two corps was assigned an armored cavalry regiment. These had three armored cavalry squadrons that were mixed formations of Abrams tanks and M3 Bradley CFVs (Cavalry Fighting Vehicles) as described in more detail below.

The M1A1 was the principal type of Abrams tank in the KTO, armed with a 120mm gun. Two battalions of the 2nd Brigade, 1st Armored Division

The backbone of the US Army tank units was the M1A1 Abrams tank. This is an example from the 3rd Brigade, 1st Armored Division during the VII Corps advance into the Iraqi desert in late February 1991.

still operated the older M1 or M1IP versions armed with the 105mm gun. The M1A1 could fire the new M829A1 APFSDS (Armor-Piercing Fin-Stabilized Discarding Sabot) projectile, popularly called the "Silver Bullet." This could defeat the armor of any Iraqi tank, including its best types such as the T-72M1. At the same time, its new multi-layer armor was invulnerable to the tank ammunition available to the Iraqi tanks in the frontal quadrant. Another significant advantage was its thermal imaging sight that enabled the tank gunner to spot enemy tanks, even in night and poor weather conditions where traditional tank sights were blind.

The M2 Bradley IFV (Infantry Fighting Vehicle) was a considerable step forward from the old M113 armored personnel carrier. While the M113 was limited to a single exposed .50 cal machine gun, the Bradley had a turret with a 25mm automatic cannon and a twin TOW antitank missile launcher. The M3 Cavalry Fighting Vehicle (CFV) was essentially similar to the M2 IFV but lacked the infantry firing ports in the rear hull and carried a five-man scout section instead of the nine-man infantry squad. The Bradleys originally deployed to the KTO were the baseline versions, including M2, M2A1, M3, and M3A1. The newer M2A2 and M3A2 versions were in production with enhanced armor protection and 692 were delivered to the KTO before the outbreak of the ground campaign, constituting about a third of the 2,200 Bradleys in theater.

A significant enhancement to US Army firepower was the new M270 Multiple Rocket Launcher System. It was dubbed "Steel Rain" and a total of 189 were deployed during *Desert Storm*.

Divisional troops usually included an armored cavalry squadron that served in the traditional cavalry role of scouting and flank security. The squadron typically included 38 M3 Bradley CFVs, 41 M1A1 tanks, six M106 4.2in self-propelled mortars, and eight M109 155mm self-propelled howitzers.

Divisional artillery in the heavy maneuver divisions included three direct-support field artillery battalions with 24 M109 155mm self-propelled howitzers each. These were generally deployed as one battalion per brigade. The division artillery also had a general support battery and a target acquisition battery. The general support battery was equipped with nine MLRSs. The M270 MLRS launcher vehicle could fire 12 M77 228mm rockets to a range of 32km. These rockets contained 644 anti-personnel and anti-armor sub-munitions. A full salvo of rockets would blanket an area of 30 acres. It was dubbed "Steel Rain" during the conflict due to its devastating effects in the open desert. A total of 189 of these rocket launchers were deployed during *Desert Storm*. The target acquisition battery had three TPQ-36 mortar locating radars, two TPQ-37 artillery locating radars, and one TPS-25 ground surveillance radar. These were used to locate Iraqi artillery batteries to destroy them with counter-battery fire.

Aside from the traditional arms such as tanks, infantry, cavalry, and artillery, the US Army divisions also included an aviation brigade. Typically, this included a battalion of AH-64 Apache attack helicopters, an assault helicopter company with 15 UH-60 Blackhawks, a command aviation company with six OH-58 Kiowas, six UH-1 Hueys, and three EH-60 Quickfix electronic warfare helicopters. The Apache battalion consisted of three companies of Apaches and a scout company of OH-58 Kiowas for a total of 18 AH-64s, 13 OH-58s, and three UH-60s. The airborne brigade provided a flexible force that enhanced the traditional armored and infantry units. The army also deployed the older AH-1F Cobra attack helicopters with 145 in cavalry units in the KTO.

The airborne divisions each had their own configuration, with the 82nd Airborne Division having a paratroop orientation while the 101st Airborne Division was helicopter-mobile. Both divisions were based around three light infantry brigades, each with three light infantry battalions. Since there was no intention to deliver the 82nd Airborne Division by air, it was configured as a vehicle-mounted light infantry formation with extensive use of HMMWV vehicles, and supported by the 3-73rd Armor, equipped with M551A1 Sheridan light tanks. The 101st Airborne Division (Air Assault) was used as intended for delivery by helicopter.

The two Marine divisions in the I MEF were reinforced beyond their TO&E and were generally organized into multiple combined-arms task forces mixing Marine battalions with tank and specialized support. Since their mission was to overcome the initial Iraqi border defenses, special attention was paid to obstacle breaching. The breaching forces were reinforced with mine rakes and mine plows, tank-mounted dozer blades, and mine-clearing line charges.

The AH-64 Apache attack helicopter saw its combat debut with US Army Aviation units in the Gulf War, with about 275 deployed. They were extensively used to conduct deep attacks, raids, and armed reconnaissance missions. This Apache is seen during a training flight over Saudi Arabia in October 1990, during Operation *Desert Shield*.

During Operation *Desert Storm*, the US Army deployed 489 UH-60 Blackhawks to the KTO serving in 18 assault helicopter companies, as well as in numerous other cavalry squadrons and other helicopter units.

A M60A1 tank of Company D, Marine 2nd Tank Battalion training for its mission as part of Task Force Breach Alpha prior to the start of the Operation *Desert Storm* ground campaign. The tank is fitted with Appliqué Armor reactive armor and an M9 bulldozer kit.

Many key Marine weapons were different from their army counterparts. The Marines' principal tank was the M60A1 with the M60A1 (RISE Passive) being the main variant. Many of these were upgraded with Appliqué Armor, a type of explosive reactive armor, before the start of the ground campaign. The Marines had planned to replace their M60A1 tanks with the new M1A1 Abrams, but few had arrived by 1990, only enough to equip two companies of the Marine Reserve 4th Tank Battalion. The Marine 2nd Tank Battalion received M1A1 tanks from the army. In total, the USMC deployed 76 M1A1 tanks and 353 M60A1 tanks in the KTO.

Due to their traditional amphibious mission, the US Marine Corps used the AAVP-7A1 (Assault Amphibian Vehicle) as their primary armored transporter. This had a crew of three plus 21 Marine troops, and so was considerably larger than the army's Bradley. It had a small turret with either a .50 cal machine gun or a combined .50 cal machine gun and 40mm automatic grenade launcher, depending on variant. In comparison to the Bradley, it had less firepower and less armor, since its primary mission was to put the Marines ashore during an amphibious landing. There were 473 AAVP-7A1s deployed to the KTO, as well as 59 command and recovery sub-variants. The Marines had additional vehicles afloat.

The US Marines deployed four squadrons of the new AH-1W Super Cobra attack helicopters during Operation *Desert Storm*. The AH-1W helicopters were credited with the destruction of 97 tanks, 104 APCs, and numerous other targets during the conflict.

The Marine Light Armored Infantry battalions were intended for the reconnaissance, security, and economy-of-force missions. They were equipped with the LAV (Light Armored Vehicle), a lightly armored, eight-wheeled transporter. The basic type was the LAV-25 armed with the same 25mm gun as the army's Bradley. The LAV-25 had a crew of three plus four scouts for dismounted missions. There were other specialized versions including an antitank vehicle with TOW missiles (LAV-AT), 81mm mortar (LAV-M), logistics (LAV-L), command-and-control (LAV-C2), and recovery (LAV-R). There were 372 LAVs deployed to the KTO, of which 193 were the basic LAV-25 and the remainder were the specialized types.

Marine aviation also differed from its army counterpart. Its primary attack helicopter force consisted of four squadrons of AH-1W Super Cobra and two squadrons of the older AH-1J Sea Cobra helicopters. The standard Marine utility helicopter consisted of different variants of the UH-1 Huey and the CH-46 Sea Knight as the principal transport helicopters.

By way of comparison, about half of the active army's combat power was deployed to Operation *Desert Storm* compared to about 85 percent of the active Marine Corps forces. US troops totaled 540,331 or roughly 68 percent of the total Coalition forces.

The backbone of the British 1st Armoured Division was the Challenger Mk.3 main battle tank. This is one from the Royal Scots Dragoon Guards, 7th Armoured Brigade, alongside the Basra–Kuwait City Highway on February 28, 1991.

Company C, 1st Battalion, The Staffordshire Regiment, 1st Armoured Division during a live fire training exercise to assault a trench complex on January 6, 1991.

European forces

The two most significant European armies to take part in the campaign were those of Britain and France. The principal element of the British forces during Operation *Granby* was the 1st Armoured Division that served in VII Corps. This was a full-strength armored division based around the 4th and 7th Armoured Brigades. These were combined-arms formations consisting of armored and mechanized infantry units. An armored regiment battle group typically would have an attached mechanized infantry company with Warrior IFVs, while the mechanized infantry battalion battle group had an attached tank squadron with Challenger tanks. For example, in the 4th Armoured Brigade, the 14/20 King's Hussars (-) had a company of the Grenadier Guards while the Royal Scots had an attached tank squadron from the Life Guards.

The three armored regiments in the division had one of two configurations with either 43 or 58 Challenger tanks. The Queen's Royal Irish Hussars and the Royal Scots Dragoon Guards had 58, while the 14/20 King's Hussars

The Warrior infantry fighting vehicle was used by British mechanized infantry units such as this one from 1st Battalion, The Staffordshire Regiment, 1st Armoured Division in Saudi Arabia shortly before the outbreak of the ground campaign.

had 43. These regiments also used the Scorpion CVR-T (Combat Vehicle Reconnaissance-Tracked) for reconnaissance. A total of 226 Challenger Mk.3 main battle tanks were deployed to the KTO, of which 52 were replacements.

The division's mechanized infantry was equipped with the Warrior IFV. The Warrior was roughly comparable to the US Army's Bradley. It was armed with a 30mm automatic cannon and had a crew of three, and an embarked infantry section in the rear of up to seven troops. Armored cavalry squadrons used the Scimitar CVR(T) as well as the Striker variant armed with Swingfire antitank missiles. The older FV432 APC was used in a variety of utility roles. The Royal Artillery regiments of the Divisional Artillery Group had batteries of the M109A1 155mm self-propelled howitzer, M110 203mm self-propelled howitzer, and MLRS artillery rocket launchers. Army Air Corps squadrons used the Gazelle and Lynx helicopters.

The French component for Operation *Daguet* was Division Daguet, serving with the XVIII Airborne Corps. This was based around the 6e Division Légère Blindée (6th Light Armored Division) based in Nîmes, with attached units from other divisions. It was essentially an expedient mechanized cavalry division, divided into two brigade headquarters (Poste de commandement) designated as PC Rouge (Red) and PC Vert (Green). The division had only a single tank regiment, the 4e Régiment de dragons, with 44 AMX-30B2 tanks as part of PC Vert. The AMX-30B2 had been modernized prior to the war with a thermal imaging sight, but it was relatively antiquated and lightly armored compared to the Abrams and Challenger, since the new Leclerc main battle tank had not yet arrived in service. The armored cavalry units used the AMX-10RC and ERC-90 armored cars, while the infantry used VAB wheeled armored personnel carriers. The two army aviation regiments used the Gazelle and Puma helicopters.

Panhard ERC-90 Sagaie armored car of the 1er Régiment de hussards parachutistes of Division Daguet.

Arab ground forces

Saudi Arabia organized a large contingent of forces from numerous neighboring Arab states as well as allied Islamic states from further afield such as Pakistan. These served primarily in the two JFCs. Many of these commitments were symbolic, with the units seeing little if any fighting. In total, the JFC amounted to 185,351 troops or roughly 23 percent of the combined force.

The Saudi armed forces committed a variety of units from both the Royal Saudi Land Forces (RSLF) and the Saudi Arabian National Guard (SANG). The SANG was founded as the successor to the Ikhwan, the tribal army of King Abdulaziz that had helped to defeat the Ottoman army during World War I. The SANG was intended as a link between the tribes and the royal house of Saud, protecting the royal family, guarding against military coups, guarding strategic facilities and resources, and providing security for the religious centers of Mecca and Medina. The SANG reported to the Ministry of the National Guard. The SANG began to mechanize starting in 1975, contracting training and equipment from US firms under the supervision of the OPM-SANG (Office of the Program Manager). Two motorized infantry brigades were organized, the Imam Mohammed bin Saud (IMBSB) in Riyadh and the King Abdulaziz Brigade (KAAB) in Dammam. They consisted of four combined arms battalions with V-150 armored vehicles each, a towed artillery battalion, and support elements. The hallmark vehicle of the SANG was the Cadillac-Gage V-150, with over a thousand in service in at least ten different configurations.

The RSLF constituted the regular Saudi Army and was subordinate to the Ministry of Defense and Aviation (MODA). The 4th Armored Brigade, stationed at Tabuk in the northwest, was formed starting in 1970 and based on French equipment including 290 AMX-30S tanks and AMX-10P IFV. The 8th Armored Brigade, stationed at Khamis Mushayt in the southwest, was formed in the late 1970s and equipped with US vehicles including M60A1 and M60A3 tanks, and M113 armored personnel carriers. Each MODA armored brigade had an armored reconnaissance company, three tank battalions with 35 tanks each, a mechanized infantry battalion, and an artillery battalion with 18 self-propelled guns. The five RSLF mechanized

The most common French armored vehicle in Division Daguet was the VAB (Véhicule de l'Avant Blindé) armored personnel carrier, with 214 deployed. Some of these were the VAB HOT Mephisto tank destroyer version, armed with HOT antitank missiles.

An AMX-30 GCT AuF1 155mm self-propelled gun of the Saudi 20th Armored Brigade on exercise near the Kuwaiti frontier in December 1990, immediately before the war. The vehicles next to it are an AMX-10PC command vehicle and an AMX-10RAV ammunition resupply vehicle. These vehicles were purchased from France in the early 1980s.

27

A section of M113 armored personnel carriers of the Egyptian 4th Armored Division in Saudi Arabia in December 1990 prior to the start of the ground campaign. They carry the division's lion insignia on the hull side.

The Kuwaiti 35th Mechanized Brigade was reequipped before the outbreak of the ground campaign, with Yugoslav M-84AB tanks and Soviet BMP-2 infantry fighting vehicles. Due to its similarity to Iraqi equipment, the Kuwaiti vehicles like this BMP-2 were heavily marked with added identification markings to prevent incidents of friendly fire.

brigades had an armored reconnaissance company, a tank battalion with 40 tanks, three mechanized infantry battalions with IFVs/APCs, and an artillery battalion with 18 self-propelled guns. There were also a light infantry brigade and an airborne brigade.

The largest single Arab contingent was the Egyptian 2 Corps under Maj. Gen. Salah Halabi, which deployed two divisions. Egypt was the first country to provide a major force to defend Saudi Arabia, with a mechanized division deployed north of Hafr al-Batin by mid-October 1990. The Egyptian corps eventually constituted the principal element of JFC-North. These divisions used the M60A3 tank, M113 armored personnel carriers, and M109 155mm self-propelled guns.

Kuwaiti units were the third-most significant element of the Arab Coalition forces. This consisted of Kuwaiti units that retreated into Saudi Arabia in the wake of the 1990 Iraqi invasion, and units formed afterwards. Many of these brigades were only partially formed by February 1991 and so are not listed here. Kuwaiti forces retreating into Saudi Arabia in 1990 brought some equipment with them, such as Chieftain tanks. However, the 35th Brigade was reequipped with armored vehicles ordered but not delivered prior to the Iraqi invasion, including Yugoslav M-84AB tanks and Soviet BMP-2 infantry fighting vehicles.

Pakistan deployed units including the 7th Armored Brigade with Forward Forces Command Ar'ar. This force was deployed to the far west of the Coalition forces and does not appear to have taken any role in the fighting. The Syrian 9th Armoured Division formed the reserve of JFC-North but saw no combat action during the campaign.

There were numerous other Arab contingents under JFC, including units from the UAE, Qatar, Bahrain, and others. These were generally battalion-sized or smaller and so are not listed on the Orders of Battle.

The intelligence dimension

A postwar CENTCOM assessment concluded that, "Tactically, no commander in the history of warfare has had a more comprehensive infusion of intelligence or a better picture of the enemy he faced." Ironically, the availability of so much intelligence capability led field commanders to demand more and better intelligence in a timelier fashion. The eventual means of distributing this massive flood of data was the Joint Intelligence Center (JIC).

The Gulf War was the first conflict to make use of comprehensive space-based systems. The Coalition enjoyed broad advantages in intelligence due largely to American aviation and space assets. The space-based assets included a broad range of electro-optical, radar, signals intelligence (SIGINT) satellites for collecting data on the Iraqi armed forces, managed by the National Reconnaissance Office (NRO).

Nevertheless, these advanced systems were far from infallible. An NRO history noted that "the war showed that NRO systems, which had been optimized to monitor arms control agreements [with the Soviet Union], were often ill-suited to support combat operations." During Congressional testimony after the war, Gen. Schwarzkopf noted that damage assessments of air strikes against Iraqi forces were "one of the major areas of confusion" since CIA and DIA analysts underestimated bomb damage by Coalition air strikes, causing him to err too often on the side of caution as the battle evolved. Schwarzkopf also complained that intelligence arrived too slowly and imagery "was often late, unsatisfactory, or unusable" and failed to provide near real-time coverage.

To some extent, shortcomings in strategic intelligence collection were overcome using operational-tactical intelligence means. Among the first systems deployed to Saudi Arabia in the late summer of 1990 were USAF E-3B AWACS (Airborne Warning and Control System) and its naval counterpart, the E-2C Hawkeye. These systems could monitor Iraqi air activity over Kuwait and Iraq. By early 1991, the AWACS provided 24-hour coverage with five continual orbits from Saudi Arabia and Turkey. The U-2R and TR-1 reconnaissance aircraft could be fitted with a variety of electro-optical, radar, and SIGINT sensors, providing a timelier and more flexible source of intelligence. The USAF RC-135 Rivet Joint was an electronic surveillance aircraft that began operating in the KTO starting in August 1990. Among its capabilities was monitoring the electronic emissions of the Iraqi KARI air defense network and monitoring Iraqi military communications.

The E-8 JSTARS was a new and unproven intelligence system at the time of the Gulf War. It was fitted with an APY-7 side-scanning radar in the fairing below the fuselage that enabled it to detect and track moving ground targets such as tanks and vehicles. (US Air National Guard by 1st Lt. Dustin Cole)

One of the newest systems used during *Desert Storm*, and one with immediate tactical implications for the ground campaign, was the E-8A JSTARS (Joint Surveillance Target Attack Radar System). This was a C-135 reconfigured to carry an advanced APY-7 side-scanning radar to track ground targets, especially tanks and other vehicles. It was originally developed to monitor Warsaw Pact mechanized forces in Europe but was ideally suited for operations in the KTO. Although still in prototype form, two aircraft were operated from Saudi Arabia. They generally flew an orbit in the southern KTO to monitor Iraqi mechanized formations, and a second on the Iraq–Jordan border to monitor Iraqi Scud missile operations. The JSTARS was uniquely valuable since its radar was able to penetrate the cloud cover and smoke that often obscured the battlefield over Kuwait and Iraq. The Iraqi Army was largely unaware of its capabilities and believed that the poor weather over the KTO in February 1991, along with the smoke and fires initiated in late February, would effectively blind Coalition image collection over the battlefield.

At the tactical level, there were numerous other intelligence collection systems. For example, the US Army operated the OV-1 Mohawk and RC-12 Guardrail surveillance aircraft while the Marines operated the KC-130 Senior Warrior. The navy had a broad range of aircraft including the P-3C Orion, S-3 Viking, and EA-6B Prowler that had secondary intelligence collection capabilities.

Besides the NRO's space-based intelligence collection systems, the US Air Force's Space Command operated a wide range of other types of military satellites. These included the DSP (Defense Support Program) missile warning satellites, DMSP (Defense Meteorological Satellite Program) weather satellites, LANDSAT multi-spectral land-mapping satellites, and most notably, the new GPS (Global Positioning System) navigation satellites. Communication satellites such as the DSCS (Defense Satellite Communications System) and ground terminals managed by the Joint Communications Support Element (JCSE) enabled the US military to coordinate around the globe in real-time. Some of these systems offered revolutionary new capabilities. This was the first war in which GPS navigation data was available, allowing army units to move across desolate desert terrain with precision. Prior to the outbreak of the war, US units were issued with 5,330 GPS receivers, 84 percent of which were commercial equipment. The effectiveness of US intelligence systems was further enhanced by existing interfaces with allied countries that had been created before the Gulf War, most notably within NATO.

In spite of this imposing array of high-tech systems, basic intelligence assessments remained controversial up to the start of the ground campaign, particularly regarding the human element of the conflict. The most critical question was "Would the Iraqi soldier fight?" Many intelligence analysts argued that the Iraqi Army was battle-hardened and experienced. As will be discussed below, the initial contact with the Iraqi Army during the Battle of Khafji raised serious doubts about this assessment. Nevertheless, the prewar tendency to exaggerate the effectiveness of the Iraqi Army strongly influenced Coalition planning and tactics.

ORDERS OF BATTLE

IRAQI ARMED FORCES IN THE KUWAIT THEATER, FEBRUARY 1991*

2nd al-Yarmik Corps   Maj. Gen. Ibrahim Abd al-Sattar Muhammad

19th Jutaiba Infantry Division
22nd Infantry Division
23rd Shibani Infantry Division
34th Haresh Infantry Division
39th Musa ibn Nusayr Infantry Division
46th Infantry Division
56th Infantry Division
al-Amuriyah Counter-Attack Force
17th Armored Division
51st Mechanized Division

3rd Qadisiyah Corps   Maj. Gen. Salah Aboud Mahmoud

7th al-Mansur Infantry Division
8th al-Muthanna Infantry Division
11th Miqdad Infantry Division
14th al-Hamzah Infantry Division
15th al-Farouk Infantry Division
18th Tareq ibn Ziyad Infantry Division
29th Sharhabil Infantry Division
42nd Fatakh al-Futukh Infantry Division
Qadisiyah Counter-Attack Force
3rd Saladin Armored Division
5th Mohammed al-Kasem Mechanized Division

4th al-Hattin Corps   Maj. Gen. Iyad Khalil Zaki

16th Dhu al-Faqir Infantry Division
20th Rafadain Infantry Division
21st Muslim bin Aqil Infantry Division
30th Abdallah ibn Ruaha Infantry Division
36th al-Amin Infantry Division
Counter-Attack Force
1st Abu Ubaydah Mechanized Division
6th Sa'ad Armored Division

7th al-Faw Corps   Maj. Gen Ahmad Ibrahim Hammash

25th Khudeifa Infantry Division
26th Omar bin Yasr Infantry Division
27th Sadiq Infantry Division
31st Husayn Infantry Division
45th Talkha Infantry Division
46th Infantry Division
47th Infantry Division
48th Infantry Division
49th Infantry Division
52nd Tikriti Armored Division
Jihad Counter-Attack Force
10th al-Nasr Armored Division
12th al-Nu'man Armored Division

Republican Guard Forces Corps   Lt. Gen. Aayad Futayyih al-Rawi

RGFC Counter-Attack Force
Hammurabi RGFC Armored Division
Kuwaat al-Nada'a RGFC Armored Division
Medina Manarwah RGFC Armored Division
Tawakalna al-Allah RGFC Mechanized Division
RGFC Exploitation Force
as-Saiqa RGFC Special Forces Division
Nebuchadnezzar RGFC Mechanized Division
al-Adnan RGFC Motorized Division
al-Faw RGFC Motorized Division

MULTINATIONAL COALITION FORCES IN KUWAIT THEATER FEBRUARY 1991

US Third Army (Lt. Gen. John J. Yeosock)

XVIII Airborne Corps (Lt. Gen. Gary E. Luck)
Division Daguet (French 6e DLB)
82nd Airborne Division
101st Airborne Division (Air Assault)
24th Infantry Division (Mechanized)
3rd Armored Cavalry Regiment

VII Corps (Lt. Gen. Frederick M. Franks, Jr.)
1st Armored Division
3rd Armored Division
1st Infantry Division (Mech)
1st (UK) Armoured Division
1st Cavalry Division
2nd Armored Cavalry Regiment

Joint Forces Command (Lt. Gen. Khalid bin Sultan al-Saud)

Joint Forces Command North (Maj. Gen. Sulaiman al-Wuhayyib)
Egyptian 2 Corps
3rd Mechanized Infantry Division
4th Armored Division
Task Force Khalid
Saudi 20th Mechanized Brigade
Saudi 4th King Khalid Armored Brigade
Kuwaiti 35th Mechanized Brigade
Kuwaiti 15th Infantry Brigade
Syrian 9th Armoured Division (reserve)

I Marine Expeditionary Force (Lt. Gen. Walter E. Boomer)
1st Marine Division (Reinforced)
2nd Marine Division (Reinforced)
Tiger Brigade (1st Brigade, 2nd Armored Division) (Army)

Joint Forces Command East (Maj. Gen. Sultan Adi al-Mutairi)
SANG 2nd Infantry Brigade (Mtz)
Saudi 8th King Fahd Armored Brigade
Saudi 10th King Faisal Mechanized Brigade
Kuwaiti 35th al-Fatah Brigade
Qatari Brigade

---

*Brigades of some additional divisions were sent into Kuwait in 1991 to make up for casualties during the air campaign

OPPOSING PLANS

IRAQ

The Iraqi armed forces had a difficult time developing effective plans due to Saddam's micromanagement of the planning process and the weakness of Iraqi intelligence services to accurately assess the scope and capabilities of the Coalition ground forces.

The planning process was deformed by Saddam's conviction that the battle-hardened Iraqi Army could inflict heavy losses on their inexperienced Coalition foes, and that the US Army would be unwilling to persevere in the face of such casualties. Saddam Hussein failed to anticipate the devastating effects of the Coalition air campaign. Saddam overestimated the ability of his expensive air defense network to blunt the Coalition air forces, and he lacked the technical appreciation and imagination to envision the damage that could be inflicted by air forces substantially more modern and extensive than any ever used in previous conflicts in the region.

The Iraqi General Staff formulated the plans for the defense of Kuwait based on several incorrect assumptions. They believed that the Coalition ground attack would be terrain-oriented in support of their announced strategic goal of liberating Kuwait. They were not expecting that a force-oriented attack aimed at destroying the RGFC was the Coalition's actual plan. There was also a widespread conviction that the Coalition forces could not navigate and operate in the barren desert region west of Kuwait, further reinforcing their belief that the Coalition attack would be focused on Kuwait.

The Iraqi General Staff believed that there were five likely avenues-of-approach for the Coalition attack, and the Iraqi Army was deployed accordingly. These five options were: an amphibious assault on the Kuwaiti coastline; an attack up the coastal road from Ras al-Khafji to Kuwait City; an attack from al-Wafrah towards Kuwait City; an attack through the "Elbow" where the Kuwait southern border abruptly turns north; and an attack up the Wadi al-Batin, the dry riverbed on the western Kuwait border with Iraq. There was also some suspicion that the Coalition would conduct a deep airborne landing, perhaps at Safwan or in support of the amphibious landing.

The strongest Iraqi defenses were oriented to counter these five possible approaches. The initial "Line in the Sand" consisted of the Iraqi infantry divisions deployed behind obstacles and defensive works. The 2 Corps was stationed east of Kuwait City to counter an expected amphibious landing. The 3 Corps was stationed in southeastern Kuwait to block the approaches to Kuwait City along the coastal road or al-Wafrah. The 4 Corps was positioned in southwestern Kuwait to cover any approaches on the eastern side of the Wadi al-Batin. Each of these corps had a counter-attack force of two or more maneuver divisions in tactical reserve about 50km from the border, to counter-attack any Coalition penetrations of the initial echelon of infantry divisions. The strategic reserve consisted of the Republican Guard Forces Corps deployed in two echelons in a crescent pattern on the Iraqi side of Kuwait's northwestern border.

The Iraqi General Staff did not rule out the possibility of Coalition operations west of Wadi al-Batin, and so deployed the 7 Corps in this area. However, the Iraqi 7 Corps was deployed as a screening force in a much less dense concentration than the corps located in Kuwait, and their associated counter-attack force was less substantial. An officer attending a briefing of the defense plan to the entire RGFC leadership on November 23 concluded that the plan was "not convincing ... The numbers presented [of Coalition forces] were much lower than the real ones. The general plan presented for our defense was based on the conditions of our war with Iran ... as if we were going to fight the Iranian army."

The Iraqi General Staff had a realistic assessment of the limited capabilities of the Iraqi infantry divisions, and so expected to use them entrenched behind a defensive belt. Dubbed the "Saddam Line," this stretched from the Persian Gulf west along the border of Kuwait and another 40 miles (65km) along the Iraqi border of Iraq, totaling 175 miles (280km). This belt included flame trenches filled with oil, sand berms, antitank ditches, barbed wire, and minefields. The fire trenches were most common in the 4 Corps sector opposite the Egyptian 2 Corps. Each trench was about a kilometer long, consisting of ten 100m sections. Each section contained three fuel drums connected by piping to one another, as well as some reserve drums further behind. The flow of the fuel was controlled from a bunker in the rear, and the fuel was ignited electrically.

Usually, an infantry division would have a security zone several kilometers deep that was lightly patrolled by the divisional reconnaissance battalion. Behind this was the operations zone, where most of the divisional combat troops were deployed.

The Iraqi Army made extensive use of minefields in Kuwait, totaling about 7 million mines. About half of these were along the southern Kuwaiti border in two belts about 60–150m deep. Additional minefields were placed along the Gulf coast to protect against amphibious landings. About 10 percent of these mines were antitank mines while the remainder were anti-personnel mines. Aside from the ubiquitous Soviet TM-62 antitank mine, the Iraqis had large numbers of Italian Valsella mines. Likewise, about two-thirds of the anti-personnel mines were modern Italian Valmera and Valsella types. These minefields were difficult to keep concealed since they were often in open desert areas and so often exposed by winds.

The Iraqi Army had made extensive use of chemical weapons in the war with Iran. However, no chemical munitions were issued to units in Kuwait. Iraqi divisional commanders were told that chemical weapons would not be used unless the Coalition penetrated Iraqi territory. In the event, Saddam did not authorize the use of chemical weapons during the war, probably fearing that the Coalition was better prepared to employ chemical weapons and defend against them than his own forces. Most Iraqi infantry units had protective masks for their troops but no protective battledress. The chemical filtration systems fitted on Iraqi combat vehicles were in most cases worn out and non-functional and not all vehicles had such protective suites.

COALITION

Operational planning was heavily controlled by CENTCOM, nominally in coordination with the Saudi Joint Forces Command. Following the invasion of Kuwait, Saudi Arabia made the unprecedented move of permitting the basing of foreign troops on its soil. CENTCOM deployed a forward headquarters element (FHE) from Tampa, Florida, to Riyadh in August 1990. CENTCOM had unilaterally developed a plan for short-term defense of Saudi Arabia in early August 1990 in the event that the Iraqi armed forces continued their offensive across the Kuwait border into Saudi Arabia. By mid-August, a US/Saudi Joint Directorate of Planning (JDOP) was established in Riyadh to coordinate future plans. This was eventually replaced by a Coalition, Coordination, Communication, and Integration Center (C3IC) developed by US officers already in Saudi Arabia with previous experience working with the SANG.

Saudi Arabia initially asked the US to establish a linear defense along the Saudi–Kuwait border. The US favored a defense of critical ports and oil facilities and came up with a scheme to trade space for time, assuming an imminent invasion by Iraq. As the probability of an Iraqi invasion of Saudi Arabia diminished, planning began to back off from emergency scenarios.

Early CENTCOM planning assumed that the US government would cap the size of US forces in Saudi Arabia to about 150,000 troops. The early defense plan was heavily dependent on airpower, with A-10 and F-117 strike aircraft deployed in the initial waves. The US Air Force came up with an expedient airpower strike plan dubbed *Instant Thunder* to offer a counter-attack option if Iraqi forces continued across the Saudi border.

On October 11, 1990, the senior American leadership – including President George H. W. Bush, Secretary of Defense Dick Cheney, and Gen. Colin Powell – met at the White House to discuss strategic plans. There was a consensus that sanctions against Iraq alone were not sufficient to force Saddam to withdraw from Kuwait. Brig. Gen. Buster Glosson, the head of planning from CENTAF, presented the air force plans.

Schwarzkopf presented a plan for a single-corps attack into Kuwait. This was viewed skeptically by many participants, and later dubbed as "Hey diddle-diddle, up-the-middle." Powell made it clear that this was the best that could be undertaken with the available ground forces. Bush asked how long it would take to deploy a second corps and Powell responded that it could be in place by January 1, 1991. Although

US officials meet in Saudi Arabia on January 9, 1991, to discuss final plans for the ground campaign. From left to right, they are Lt. Gen. Calvin Waller, deputy chief of staff, CENTCOM; Gen. Colin Powell, chairman, Joint Chiefs of Staff; Dick Cheney, Secretary of Defense; Gen. Norman Schwarzkopf, commander-in-chief, US CENTCOM; and Paul D. Wolfowitz, Under-Secretary of Defense for Policy.

this meeting did not authorize the shift to a larger Coalition attack force, it did convince Secretary of Defense Cheney that it would be necessary.

Assistant Defense Secretary for International Security Affairs Henry Rowen oversaw the Pentagon's policies in the Middle East, and he was tasked by Cheney to examine better campaign plans. Rowen became convinced that a better option than CENTCOM's "charge of the light brigade into the wadi of death" was an additional thrust through the open desert of western Iraq. This option was presented to Cheney, who created an informal team around the former JCS J-5 (planning) Lt. Gen. Dale Vesser. He offered various options under Operation *Scorpion* including a drive out of the western desert towards Baghdad. Cheney did not like the Baghdad option but did think that the thrust from the western desert was the correct approach, which he dubbed "the Western Excursion."

In the meantime, Powell had assembled his own team at the JCS to work on a plan, favoring a multi-division attack through the western desert to destroy the Republican Guard concentration northeast of Kuwait. Schwarzkopf was angered by his reception in October in Washington DC, complaining that his presentation was only meant to offer options possible with a single corps. Schwarzkopf tasked his team of planners in Riyadh, dubbed "the Jedis," to examine a two-corps campaign, also including an operation in the western desert.

Powell visited Schwarzkopf on October 22, 1990. Although there were still some differences between the Powell/Cheney/Jedi plans, they were converging towards a common point. The issue was settled on October 31 at a National Security Council meeting called by President Bush. Powell requested a very generous reinforcement including a second army corps, doubling the Marine and air force contingents, and increasing the three carrier battle groups to six. There was a consensus on the plan, though with the proviso that the UN Security Council endorse military action as well as Saudi support for the plan. A key ingredient in the plan was to win the acquiescence of the Soviet leadership, since Moscow could block the UN endorsement.

After considerable diplomatic action, on November 29 the UN passed Resolution 678, authorizing the eviction of Iraqi forces from Kuwait by "all necessary means." Iraq was given until January 15, 1991 to withdraw from Kuwait.

The operational scheme for the XVIII Airborne Corps and VII Corps in the western desert was dubbed the "Great Wheel." These formations would initially head northward across the frontier and then wheel to the east towards Kuwait to confront the RGFC. The Coalition governments were briefed on the planning in late November and early December 1990, and by December 16, British, French, and Egyptian officers had been added to the joint planning staff.

The options for the XVIII Airborne Corps and VII Corps were broadly accepted, but the role of the I MEF remained contentious. The MARCENT command, Lt. Gen. Walter Boomer, was infuriated that the Jedi cell had been planning the operation for two months with no Marine input. The controversy came to a head at a November 6 meeting at CENTCOM, when the Jedis briefed their plan with the Marines dissenting. The Marines were critical of the army's unimaginative plan to use them as a battering ram to cover their right flank. The Marines wanted to aim for Kuwait City, advancing closer to the coast and therefore closer to their logistical support from the navy. Schwarzkopf agreed and told the Jedis to stop calling the Marine role a "fixing attack" and instead refer to it as a "main attack." Schwarzkopf delegated more authority to the MARCENT for planning their role.

Even though the US Marine Corps has a traditional mission of amphibious assault, a seaborne landing against the Kuwaiti coast was ruled out. This was in part due to the terrain features, such as the urban sprawl south of Kuwait City and the islands and marshlands on the northern coast. In addition, the coastal waters were infested with minefields and Iraq was known to have a significant coastal anti-ship missile force. Rather than conduct any amphibious landings, the Coalition plan included a deception effort to suggest planned amphibious landings to keep additional Iraqi forces tied down near the coast. This scheme was reasonably successful, with the Iraqi Army deploying the 2 Corps to cover the coast north of Kuwait City.

The original scheme to have the British 1st Armoured Division reinforce the I MEF in Kuwait was eventually switched to its participation with the VII Corps west of Wadi al-Batin. This was prompted by British planners who were far more familiar with the doctrine and tactics of the army's VII Corps from Germany than with the US Marines. In its place, the army reinforced the I MEF with a brigade from the 2nd Armored Division. The French Division Daguet was originally placed under the Saudi JFC but was later shifted to the XVIII Airborne Corps since its light mechanized configuration was better suited to the mission than an assault into Kuwait.

The initial Marine plan was to push up the coast to Kuwait City. However, this mission was already assigned to the SANG and the JFC-East command. Schwarzkopf broached the subject with Prince Khalid, the JFC commander, who rebuffed the change. As a result, the I MEF mission was aimed at the "Elbow," located between JFC-East and JFC-North. The strongest element of JFC-North was the Egyptian 2 Corps. There were some political considerations at play in the deployment of Egyptian rather than Saudi forces to the western Kuwait sector. There had been clashes between Kuwaiti and Saudi militias in the area in 1920 and the Saudis did not wish to revive old antagonisms.

Since the deadline for UN Resolution 678 was reached on January 15, 1991, President Bush authorized US military action by National Security Directive 54. The directive's stated mission was to compel the Iraqi withdrawal from Kuwait and restore Kuwait's legitimate government to promote security and stability in the Gulf. To achieve these goals, the mission of the US forces in the region was to defend Saudi Arabia and the other GCC states from attack; preclude Iraq's launching of ballistic missiles against neighboring states and forces; destroy Iraq's chemical, biological, and nuclear weapons capabilities; destroy Iraq's command-control-communications capability; and eliminate the Republican Guard as an effective fighting force. The aim of the military campaign was to drive Iraq out of Kuwait, break the will of the Iraqi Army, encourage defection of Iraqi forces, and weaken Iraqi popular support for Saddam's regime. The directive also stated that every reasonable effort should be taken to minimize US and Coalition casualties and to reduce collateral military damage to civilians and non-military infrastructure.

THE CAMPAIGN

CASUS BELLI: THE INVASION OF KUWAIT

The invasion of Kuwait was primarily undertaken by the units of the RGFC. The plan consisted of two corps-sized attacks, one emanating from the Safwan area in Iraq towards Kuwait City, and the second emanating from the desert west of Kuwait, heading south of Kuwait City and clearing the coastal region towards the Saudi border.

The Iraqi invasion began on the morning of August 2, 1990, with the seizure of border posts by Iraqi RGFC commando units. The Kuwaiti Army had been alerted to the probability of an Iraqi attack, but it was very small in comparison to the Iraqi Army, numbering about 23,000 men.

The most critical role was assigned to the Hammurabi Armored Division, which was to advance to Kuwait City. It was followed by the Nebuchadnezzar Infantry Division that was assigned to occupy the center of Kuwait City. The al-Faw Motorized Division was assigned a parallel attack further east along the Gulf coast since the terrain in the coastal zone was not well suited to an armored attack. The Tawakalna Mechanized Division was assigned to the western side of the Hammurabi Armored Division with an aim of capturing the Ali al-Salem airbase. Its secondary mission was to link up with the second western thrust. The RGFC Special Forces Brigade formed a number of special teams that infiltrated into Kuwait before the main attack in preparation for seizing key military and political objectives. The Special Forces Brigade was also used in a number of heliborne landings.

The thrust from the west was assigned to the Medina Armored Division, skirting south of the Ali al-Salem airbase and heading for the Gulf port of al-Ahmadi immediately south of Kuwait City. It was followed by the Adnan and Baghdad Divisions, which were assigned to occupy the numerous towns along the coast south of Kuwait City.

The first major clash between Iraqi and Kuwaiti forces occurred around

In response to the invasion of Kuwait, the RAF dispatched Tornado F3 fighters to Dhahran airbase to provide continuous air patrol. One is seen here taxiing out on a mission in November 1990 with a pair of US Army CH-47 Chinook helicopters evident in the background. (Author)

Iraq's invasion of Kuwait, August 2–3, 1990

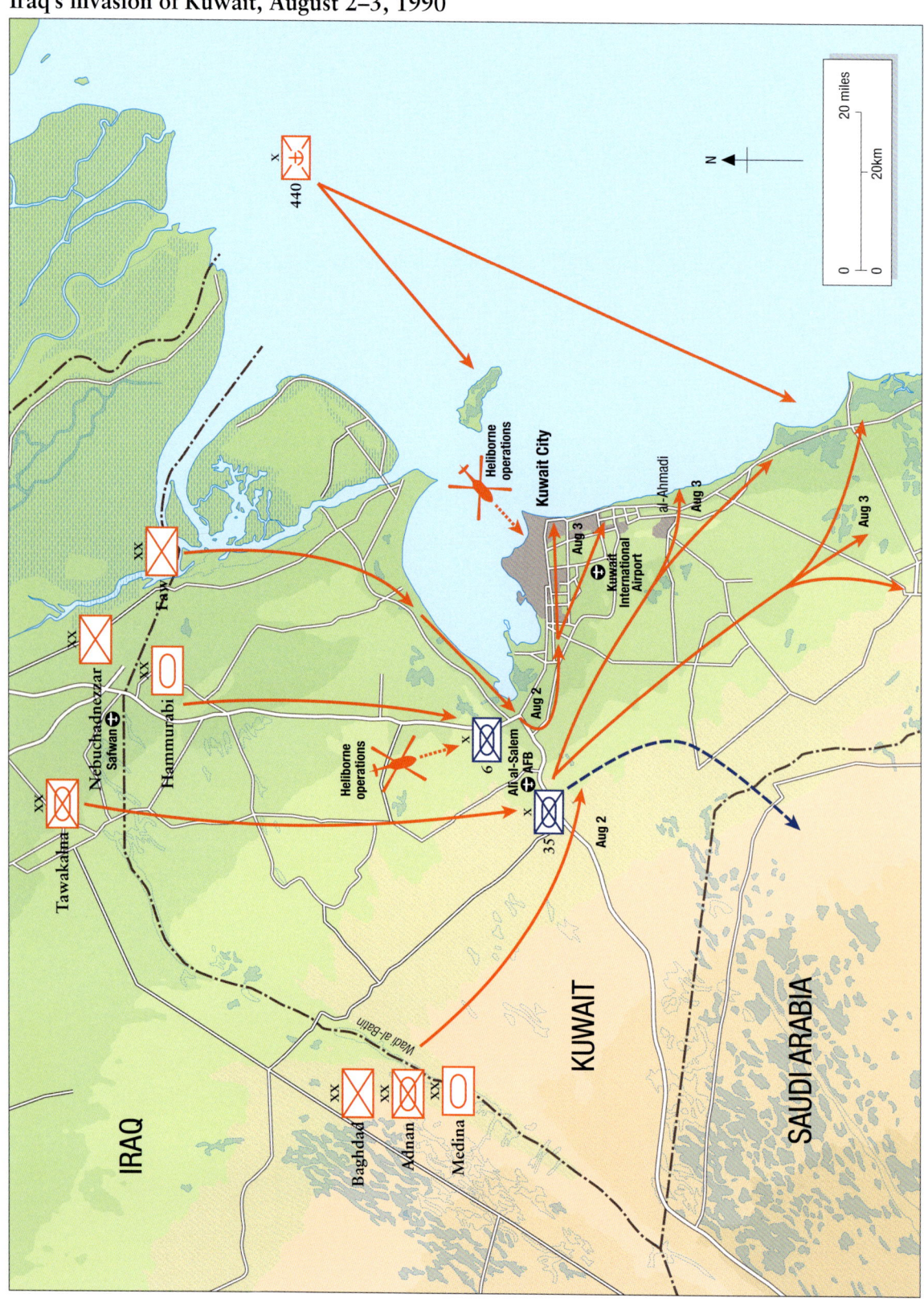

38

0600hrs when a brigade of the Hammurabi Armored Division was intercepted by a task force from the Kuwaiti 6th Mechanized Brigade equipped with Vickers tanks and BMP-2 infantry fighting vehicles. The Kuwait unit was forced aside. The Iraqi spearhead secured Mutla Pass and then encountered the lead element of the Kuwaiti 35th Mechanized Brigade advancing along the highway. The surprised Kuwaiti unit lost numerous Chieftain tanks in the encounter. Another brief tank battle occurred between the same opponents when the Hammurabi Division seized Kuwait International Airport. The main impediment to the Iraqi advance proved to be the chaos on the roads as civilians fled the city, and dwindling fuel supplies for their T-72 tanks.

The Kuwaiti 35th Mechanized Brigade proved to be much more effective in delaying the advance of the Medina Division from the west, and as a result the Medina did not reach its objective at al-Ahmadi until August 3. The military campaign was largely over by August 3. The Iraqi forces suffered very modest losses. The commando forces lost a number of teams when their helicopters were shot down, and the Baghdad Division suffered some losses from a bombing attack by Kuwaiti A-4 Skyhawks. The Hammurabi Division lost only 99 killed, 249 wounded, and 15 missing.

In the following months, Iraq consolidated its invasion and attempted to extend Baath Party control over its newest province. The invasion was condemned by a UN Security Council resolution on August 2, and the prospects for some type of international response began to emerge. Traditional Iraqi patrons such as the Soviet Union expressed their displeasure. The United States, Saudi Arabia, and many European countries adamantly condemned the attack.

The Iraqi General Military Intelligence Directorate (GMID) on August 12 issued a report warning that in the short term, air attacks against Iraq were more likely than ground operations. A follow-on report on August 14 noted that preparations for a ground attack would take time and that American pronouncements strongly suggested the intention of the Bush administration to take military action. By August 23, the GMID was warning Baghdad to conduct defensive preparations in Kuwait as promptly as possible.

Saddam began to initiate a broad series of defensive measures to resist any future Coalition military action. The threat of air attack led to instructions to disperse major army formations and to make the air defense forces ready

The US response to the Iraqi invasion of Kuwait was dubbed *Desert Shield*. It involved a substantial transfer of troops and equipment to Saudi Arabia, such as this US Army engineer unit recently disembarked from a C-5A transporter at Dhahran airbase in November 1991. (Author)

for war. Passive defense measures were accelerated, such as sending 689 derelict tanks and armored vehicles to Kuwait to act as decoys, reduction in military radio transmissions, and construction of numerous fortifications in both Iraq and Kuwait to resist air attack. In September 1990, Saddam outlined the Tariq Project, a scheme to use oil for defensive purposes. Besides the fire trenches mentioned previously, there was also a scheme to create a fire barrier along the Kuwait coast and Bubiyan Island, as well as a major oil spill in the Gulf. Experiments were conducted to determine whether oil fires could be used to defeat observation from aircraft and satellites.

Through the autumn of 1990, the RGFC units that had been involved in the initial invasion were pulled back from Kuwait and deployed in the Safwan area to act as a theater reserve for any future conflict. In their place, divisions of the regular Iraqi Army were deployed to Kuwait as described previously.

Iraqi buildup in KTO

	Aug 20, 1990	Nov 8, 1990	Dec 18, 1990
Troops	54,865	400,000	500,000
Tanks	848	3,600	4,100
APC/IFV	603	2,300	2,580
Artillery	342	1,300	2,830
Divisions	4	27	32

The final GMID assessment on December 26, 1990 outlined three possible Coalition attack plans. The first expected an initial attack against the high command posts, with subsequent actions dependent on the results of the first attack and the reaction of Iraqi troops. The second expected intensive air and missile attacks against a broad range of strategic targets, followed by bombardment of Iraqi troops deployed in Kuwait, and finally a rapid advance into Kuwait; this was close to the actual Coalition plan in broad outlines. The third expected a simultaneous air, missile, land, and naval attack. Even at this late date, the GMID had failed to appreciate the buildup of the XVIII Airborne Corps and VII Corps. In the final meetings with Saddam on January 15, 1991, an Iraqi officer later recalled that there was an air of collective denial among the senior leaders that the war would start at all.

The Saddam Line was a network of minefields, obstacles, and defensive strongpoints erected by Iraqi Army engineers along the Kuwait–Saudi border in the autumn and winter of 1990. This is an example facing the 1st Marine Division on the opening day of the ground campaign, with burning oil wells visible in the background.

The Tariq Project was a multi-faceted scheme to use oil as a weapon. On February 22, the Iraqi Army began setting fire to oil wells in Kuwait in the hopes that the resulting fire and smoke would obscure the battlefield from Coalition surveillance aircraft and satellites. This is an example near the al-Wafrah plantation.

THE AIR CAMPAIGN

The Coalition air campaign began at 0200hrs on January 17 with an attack by AH-64 Apache helicopters to destroy Iraqi early-warning radars near the border. The initial wave of attacks was focused on the suppression of enemy air defenses (SEAD), especially the French-supplied KARI air defense command-and-control system. This included air attacks on strategic command posts, Iraqi Air Force headquarters, air defense missile and radar sites, and airbases. Another priority was the destruction of sites associated with weapons-of-mass-destruction (WMD) such as the Project 777 nuclear weapons development site at Tuwaitha and the chemical warfare labs at al-Samarra. (A detailed assessment of the air campaign is provided in Osprey Air Campaign 25 Desert Storm *1991*. This abbreviated account focuses on its impact on the ground campaign.)

The focus of the air campaign began to shift during the third week of the campaign, from January 31 to February 5, from attacks against strategic targets in Iraq to attacks on the Iraqi Army in the KTO. This phase of the air campaign was aimed at "preparing the battlefield" for the eventual ground campaign, with a goal of reducing Iraqi capabilities in the KTO by 50 percent. The initial air attacks were aimed at a variety of targets, including logistics hubs, troop concentrations, and border defenses. A total of 41 of 54 highway bridges between Iraq and Kuwait were dropped, as well as 31 pontoon brigades that had been erected as replacements. The air attacks dropped the Iraqi Army's rate of supply from 216,000 tons per day to only 20,000 tons. The supply situation was worsened by the extensive loss of trucks to air attack.

In one of his more bizarre decisions, on January 21, Saddam ordered air defense units to cut down on their use of ammunition and missiles against Coalition aircraft to conserve them for a protracted war. After the war, Iraqi officers complained that these orders triggered the gradual collapse of morale since they were not permitted to fire back.

One of the stars of the air campaign was the F-117A strike fighter. It was used in the initial attacks on the Iraqi air defense network since its novel stealth technology made it nearly invisible to Iraqi radar.

By the beginning of February, the focus began to shift to the destruction of pinpoint targets, especially tanks, AFVs, and artillery. Air attacks using conventional unguided bombs were found to be marginally effective against such targets, leading to a shift to precision munitions. The A-10 attack aircraft began using large numbers of AGM-65 Maverick guided missiles, while F-111 strike aircraft began to engage in "tank plinking" using laser-guided Paveway bombs. This led to a dramatic increase in kill claims against Iraqi weapons in the KTO as shown on the accompanying chart.

Degradation of Iraqi weapons strength in the KTO *(cumulative losses)*

Jan 22	14	0	77
Jan 27	65	50	281
Feb 01	476	243	356
Feb 06	728	552	535
Feb 11	862	692	771
Feb 16	1,439	879	1,271
Feb 21	1,563	887	1,426
Feb 23	1,688	929	1,452
Feb 24	1,772	948	1,474
Original strength	**4,280**	**2,880**	**3,100**

The B-52 Stratofortress flew over 1,600 missions during *Desert Storm*, dropping 27,000 tons of munitions, a third of all the munitions delivered during the air campaign.

A tactical consequence of the "tank plinking" was that Iraqi tank crews soon avoided manning their tanks during the daytime due to the air threat. Instead, they dug revetments away from the tank. This situation continued after the start of the air campaign, with the result that Iraqi tanks were often unmanned when Coalition troops first appeared.

Postwar interviews with Iraqi prisoners-of-war found that the two most feared aircraft were the A-10 attack aircraft and B-52 bomber. The B-52 bomber attacks were by far the most dreaded form of air attack due to the devastating impact of dozens of bombs in a small area. The A-10 was dubbed "the silent gun" by some Iraqi units because its turbofan engines were not as noisy as other jet aircraft, and it would appear unexpectedly out of low cloud cover. The arrival of A-10 aircraft overhead was dreaded by

Iraqi soldiers since they loitered over the area and repeatedly attacked. The commander of the 50th Armored Brigade of the 12th Armored Division "explained that he did not want his tanks to fire indiscriminately at the A-10s because they would give away their positions. He remarked wryly that he did not have difficulty enforcing this order."

This 52nd Brigade of the 52nd Armored Division was singled out for air attack due to its proximity to the intended VII Corps breach. Lt. Gen. Franks, the VII Corps commander, pointed to it on a map and told his staff "to make it go away." By the start of the ground campaign, the "Go Away Brigade" lost 90 tanks and AFVs with only 15 T-55 tanks and 15 BMP-1s remaining; half of its troops deserted. The 50th Armored Brigade, 12th Armored Division reported moving two mechanized battalions on February 25, when eight A-10s showed up and proceeded to destroy 20 APCs and three tanks and caused enough damage to others to render both battalions combat-ineffective. A VII Corps postwar report noted that:

Iraqi soldiers feared the A-10, since it would loiter and attack Iraqi positions for many minutes. This is an A-10 of the 74th Tactical Fighter Squadron, 23rd Tactical Fighter Wing, based at King Fahd airbase in November 1990. (Author)

> Iraqi soldiers became uniformly afraid of air raids. Attracting attention was a serious mistake. Whether it was moving on the roads, sleeping in armored vehicles, using a radio, or defending a position with AAA [anti-aircraft artillery], all activities resulted in a likely attack by air. Very little could be accomplished; most time was spent just trying to survive. Even for combat veterans [of the Iran–Iraq War] the bombing was the worst thing they had experienced in combat. The Iraqi war-weariness going into the war, combined with the air campaign, destroyed the will to fight in many soldiers and units. Relief for most of the front-line divisions came with the start of the ground campaign which offered them their first chance to surrender.

The material effects of the air campaign on the Iraqi Army were substantial. The early attacks on the army's supply network in Kuwait led to widespread shortages of food and supplies. The infantry divisions along the Kuwait–Saudi border were the most badly affected and by late February lacked food and water. The intense bombardment and the dreadful conditions in the forward units led to widespread desertion. Postwar interrogations found that the causes of desertion were war-weariness, lack of conviction in the cause, and the devastation caused by the air campaign. Some examples from the unit encountered by the VII Corps west of Wadi al-Batin are listed in the accompanying chart. The VII Corps estimated that the Iraqi infantry divisions opposing them had an initial strength on average of 7,500 men that was reduced to only 4,100 by the start of the ground campaign due to desertions and casualties from air attack and artillery fire.

Examples of Iraqi desertions in the KTO

	Corps	Initial strength	Desertions
27th Infantry Division	7	8,120	4,000
48th Infantry Division	7	5,000	1,000
50th Armored Brigade	7	1,800	360
52nd Armored Brigade	7	1,125	550
Hammurabi Division	RGFC	10,000	5,000

MISSILE WAR

The Iraqi Air Force had little capability to conduct retaliatory air strikes against the Coalition. An attempted mission on January 25, 1991, by two Iraqi Mirage F-1s to strike the Saudi oil export terminal at Ras Tanura failed when the aircraft were shot down by Saudi F-15C fighters. Saddam placed greater faith in the ability of his ballistic missile force to conduct deep attacks than conventional aircraft attack. The Iraqi Air Force was so ineffective in the first week of the war that, on January 26, Saddam ordered surviving aircraft evacuated to its erstwhile enemy Iran.

Curiously enough, the first missile target was not Saudi Arabia but Israel. Saddam hoped that his missile strikes into Israel would result in retaliatory Israeli air strikes into Iraq. He expected that any such strikes would cause Arab members of the Coalition to question their role in the war and undermine the cohesion of the Coalition.

An initial missile launch against Israel was planned for August 1990 and ten al-Husayn missiles were fueled on August 8. However, Saddam decided against a missile strike until after Iraq was attacked by the Coalition. On the morning of January 17, Saddam telephoned the commander of Brigade 224, Gen. Hazim Abd al-Razzaq al-Ayyubi, and ordered him to begin attacking the "criminal Zionist entity with the heaviest fire possible." At the time, Brigade 224 was deployed in the western Iraqi desert along with the partially equipped Brigade 223. When the air campaign began on January 17, the missile fixed sites of Brigade 223 were among the first targets of Coalition air attack.

At the start of the war, Iraq had 230 missiles, but fuel for only 118. The first al-Husayn missile attacks began in the early morning hours of January 18 with eight missiles against Tel Aviv and Haifa by Brigade 224. A single attempt to launch a missile from the new Brigade 223 failed. On January 20, the brigades were dispersed and began missile strikes against Saudi Arabia from sites in southern Iraq. In total, some 93 missiles were launched, nearly all by Brigade 224.

The Bush administration was concerned that Israel would retaliate for the missile attacks, and began negotiations with Tel Aviv to avoid this unwelcome diplomatic complication. To ease Israeli concerns, the US Army transferred Patriot missile batteries to Israel to reinforce Israeli batteries. On January 18, two Patriot batteries of the 4-43rd ADA (Air Defense Artillery) arrived in Israel followed by two batteries of the 1-7th ADA on January 25–26. Israel's first Patriot batteries reached operational status on January 21. The Dutch 327 Squadron reached Israel on February 24, but did not engage any Scuds. Patriot batteries had already been deployed in Saudi Arabia since August 1990 and eventually 21 Patriot batteries with 132 launchers were deployed there.

An M901 Patriot launcher from Bravo Battery, 2-7th ADA, 11th Air Defense Artillery Brigade. This unit was one of the first trained to deal with the ballistic missile threat and it was deployed to Dhahran, Saudi Arabia during *Desert Storm*. (Author)

Iraqi missile sites were a prime target of the air campaign. About 1,500 sorties were flown over 43 days against Scud targets including mobile launchers, fixed launch sites, suspected hiding locations, production plants, and storage facilities. About a third of 2,000 daily strategic air campaign sorties were diverted to the "Scud Hunt." Aside from aircraft missions, there was a major effort made to determine the location of Iraqi mobile launchers using the DSP satellites and radars located in neighboring countries. Coalition air crews claimed they had destroyed or damaged 80 launchers; A-10 crews alone claimed 51 Scud launchers. Later analysis of these strikes revealed that many of the claims were strikes against objects resembling the mobile launchers, especially large fuel trucks. The Iraqis insisted that none of their mobile launchers were destroyed in the war and turned over 12 9P117 TELs and seven al-Nida/al-Waleed improvised launch vehicles to the UN after the war.

Although the air attacks failed to destroy any mobile missile launchers, the intensity of the attacks forced Missile Brigade 224 to be extremely cautious in its operations. As a result, the tempo of missile launches fell after the first week of launches.

Special operations forces were brought into the Scud Hunt on February 7, mainly to convince Israel to abstain from military involvement. Britain had already been operating squadrons from the SAS in the deserts of western Iraq, and they were subsequently assigned to the Scud Hunt. The US Joint Special Operations Command (JSOC) deployed Delta Force teams, supported by Air Force Special Operations Command (AFSOC) Special Tactics Squadron. Delta Force and the SAS operated from a forward operating base at Al Jouf airbase in the northern Saudi desert. Delta was assigned to the area nicknamed "Scud Boulevard" northwest of the main Baghdad–Amman highway that included the al-Qaim phosphate mines where the Iraqis were suspected of hiding Scud launchers in caves. The SAS was assigned "Scud Alley," the southern sector around the H-2 airfield south to the Saudi border.

SCUD MISSILE LAUNCH ON ISRAEL, JANUARY 1991 (PP. 46–47)

Brigade 224 conducted its launches of the al-Husayn missile **(1)** from about seven areas, depending on the target. Most attacks against Israel were launched from the western Iraqi desert near Jordan. The 9P117 TEL (transporter-erector-launcher) vehicle **(2)** was prepared at a camouflaged location where a fueled missile was mounted to the launcher cradle using a crane. The launch site was pre-surveyed by special teams from the brigade. The TEL was usually accompanied to the launch site by several service vehicles **(3)**. The intention was to minimize the time it took from the arrival at the launch site to the time that the TEL departed, since the brigade was well aware that Coalition air units and special forces were on the hunt for the launcher vehicles. Launches usually occurred at night to minimize the visibility of the launch teams to Coalition observation **(4)**.

Delta Force teams were inserted by air using MH-60 and MH-47 helicopters of the 160th Special Operations Aviation Regiment and by MH-53J Pave Low IIIs from the 1st Special Operations Wing. Some Delta teams operated from modified HMMWVs, Fast Attack Vehicles, and motorcycles. The SAS infiltrated some of their teams into Iraq using modified "Pinkie" Land Rover columns, as well as aerial insertions from RAF Chinook helicopters. The special operations teams were assigned to set up outposts near likely Iraqi transport routes, and then to radio data to permit air strikes. The teams were often equipped with laser designators to assist the aircraft in conducting precision strikes. The SAS also disrupted Iraqi missile operations by targeting fiber optic cable and communication nodes that connected the mobile launchers with the Missile Corps headquarters. The Iraqis were soon aware of these operations from the reports of local civilians, and additional defense detachments accompanied the Scud launchers to defend against the special forces operations. In one incident, an eight-man SAS patrol, "Bravo Two Zero" from B Squadron 22 SAS, was discovered and attacked by an Iraqi defense patrol of Brigade 224 with only one SAS member escaping. Special forces units claimed the destruction of at least 11 Scud launchers. No actual Scud missile launchers or missiles were lost during these attacks, although Iraqi casualties in Brigade 224 were six killed and 48 wounded.

Of the 93 al-Husayn missiles launched during the war, 38 landed in Israel, 41 in Saudi Arabia, and two in Qatar and Bahrain; the remainder broke up in flight or during launch. Patriot missiles were used to engage missiles that were expected to impact in populated areas; missiles expected to land in empty desert were not engaged. A total of 158 Patriot missiles were fired, often more than one missile per target to increase the probability of hits. The US Army later assessed that the Patriots had been successful in 70 percent of their engagements: 80 percent in Saudi Arabia and 50 percent in Israel. The interceptions were made difficult by the shortcomings of the al-Husayn, which often broke up in its terminal phase due to manufacturing problems in its fuselage extensions. Of the Patriot intercepts, over a third (37 percent) were against missiles that had disintegrated during descent. This led to a target array containing multiple chunks of the missile.

US and Saudi troops inspect an al-Husayn ballistic missile that had been hit by a Patriot missile over Saudi Arabia. The al-Husayn was an Iraqi version of the Soviet Scud B missile with an enlarged fuselage fuel tank to extend its range.

Although overshadowed by the Scud, the Iraqi missile forces also employed the short-range 9K52 Luna-M (FROG-7) tactical rocket system during the campaign. This is a 9P113 launcher vehicle of Missile Brigade 225 captured by the I MEF with its empty launch rail badly pitted from repeated rocket launches.

There were no civilian deaths in Saudi Arabia due to al-Husayn impacts, but on February 25, an al-Husayn missile struck a warehouse in Dharan being used as a barracks by the 475th Quartermaster Group, killing 28 and seriously injuring 110 more. In Israel, two were killed by al-Husayn impacts; others died from indirect causes such as incorrect use of gas masks and heart attacks. A total of 4,100 buildings were damaged, with 28 of those buildings destroyed.

Although the Scud missile attacks are the best-known use of Iraqi missiles, the shorter-range tactical missiles also saw combat use. Brigade 225 with the Luna-M (FROG-7) sent one battalion each to the 3 Corps and 4 Corps in Kuwait, and likewise Brigade 226 sent battalions to these two corps as well. The initial targets for these missiles were Khafji and Ras al-Mishab in Saudi Arabia. The first Luna-M strike against Khafji was conducted on the morning of January 17, 1991, using three rockets, followed by further Luna-M and Astros rockets later in the day. The peak day was January 30, 1991, when 40 Luna-M missiles were fired.

IRAQI RAID AT KHAFJI

In August 1990, the RGFC formulated three plans for possible attacks into Saudi Arabia: shallow, medium, and deep. Little attention was paid to these plans until the start of the Coalition air campaign in January 1991. Saddam began to contemplate an Iraqi raid that might disrupt the Coalition ground attack and display the Iraqi Army's military prowess. The immediate motivation for the raid appears to have been Saddam's recollection that Iraq's fortunes in the war with Iran shifted in 1987 when Iraq moved from a defensive to offensive posture.

Planning for a shallow raid took place in late January, involving units from the 3 Corps and 4 Corps. The 3 Corps effort near the coast was envisioned as the main effort, while the 4 Corps attack was considered a diversionary operation to draw away Coalition air attacks.

The objective of the 3 Corps attack was the Saudi port town of Ras al-Khafji, a dozen miles south of the Kuwait border. The town had been evacuated at the start of the war since it was within Iraqi artillery range. At the time, the only Coalition forces around the town were a small US Marine and Navy SEAL detachment serving as a forward observation post, and some other scattered Saudi Marines and Coast Guard troops along the road north of the town.

The attack began at 2015hrs on January 29, with the 20th Armored Brigade of the 5th Mechanized Division as the spearhead followed by the rest of the division. After traveling about 15km into Saudi territory, the 20th Armored Brigade took up defensive positions near the town's desalinization plant to permit the reinforced 15th Mechanized Brigade to race deeper into Khafji. They reached the southern end of Khafji well after dark, around 2315hrs. There were some air attacks by AC-130 gunships and AH-1 attack helicopters against the Iraqi columns, but not enough to blunt the attack. There was a subsidiary seaborne raid consisting of commandos of the Iraqi Navy's Brigade 440 in about 15 small boats. These were intercepted by US Navy and Royal Navy aircraft and helicopters, and the commandos never reached their destination.

The JSTARS operating over Saudi Arabia was able to track and locate all of the Iraqi vehicles taking part in the Khafji raid and the associated attacks, and vector available strike aircraft and helicopters to their targets. Most of the close-air support missions in the immediate vicinity of Khafji were flown by Marine aircraft with targeting provided by Marine observers in the town, while the US Air Force conducted interdiction missions north of the town to prevent any further Iraqi reinforcements.

In the meantime, the 6th Brigade of the Iraqi 3rd Armored Division crossed into Saudi Arabia near the al-Wafrah plantation, as part of a deception operation to distract from the main attack. This column, consisting of about 50 tanks and 30 APCs, ran into Marine OP-2 (Observation Post-2). The Marine outpost engaged the column with TOW missiles and gunfire while calling in air support. Marine F/A-18s and A-6 strike aircraft, as well as Marine AH-1 attack helicopters, pummeled the Iraqi column and were joined by air force A-10s and F-16s. After two hours of constant air attacks, the remnants of the brigade straggled back across the Kuwait border around 0200hrs on January 30, leaving behind 22 destroyed tanks and AFVs burning in the desert.

The 4 Corps' part of the operation was a raid by the 34th Brigade of the 1st Mechanized Division as the spearhead, followed by the 27th Mechanized Brigade from the vicinity of the Ahmed al-Jaber airbase westwards. This attack was less vigorous than the other two. The Iraqi columns were halted by LAVs of Task Force Shepherd from the Marine 1st Light Armored Infantry Battalion near OP-4. They withdrew back to Iraqi lines around dawn on January 30 after enduring air attacks.

The attack on Saudi soil incensed Prince Khalid, who insisted that the Saudi-led JFC-East command, and not the US Marines, take the responsibility for recapturing the town. The JFC-East force in the immediate vicinity was the Abu Bakr Task Force, comprised of two battalions of the 2nd SANG Brigade, an M60A1 tank company of the 8th MODA Brigade, and attached elements of the Qatari Brigade with AMX-30 tanks. In the late afternoon of January 30, JFC-East deployed the 5-2nd SANG Brigade and the 8th MODA Brigade to the north of Khafji

THE BATTLE OF KHAFJI, JANUARY 29–FEBRUARY 1, 1991
The initial Iraqi army offensive of the campaign is repulsed by the Saudi Arabian National Guard.

COALITION
SAUDI
A. 5th Battalion, 2nd SANG Brigade
B. 7th Battalion, 2nd SANG Brigade
C. 8th Battalion, 2nd SANG Brigade
D. Tank Battalion, 8th MODA Tank Brigade
QATARI
E. Two tank companies, Qatari Brigade
USMC
F. 3rd Platoon, Company A, Marine 3rd Reconnaissance Battalion
G. Observation Post, 1st Surveillance Reconnaissance Intelligence Group
H. 1st Battalion, 12th Marines (Artillery)
I. Task Force Taro, 3rd Marines, 1st Marine Division

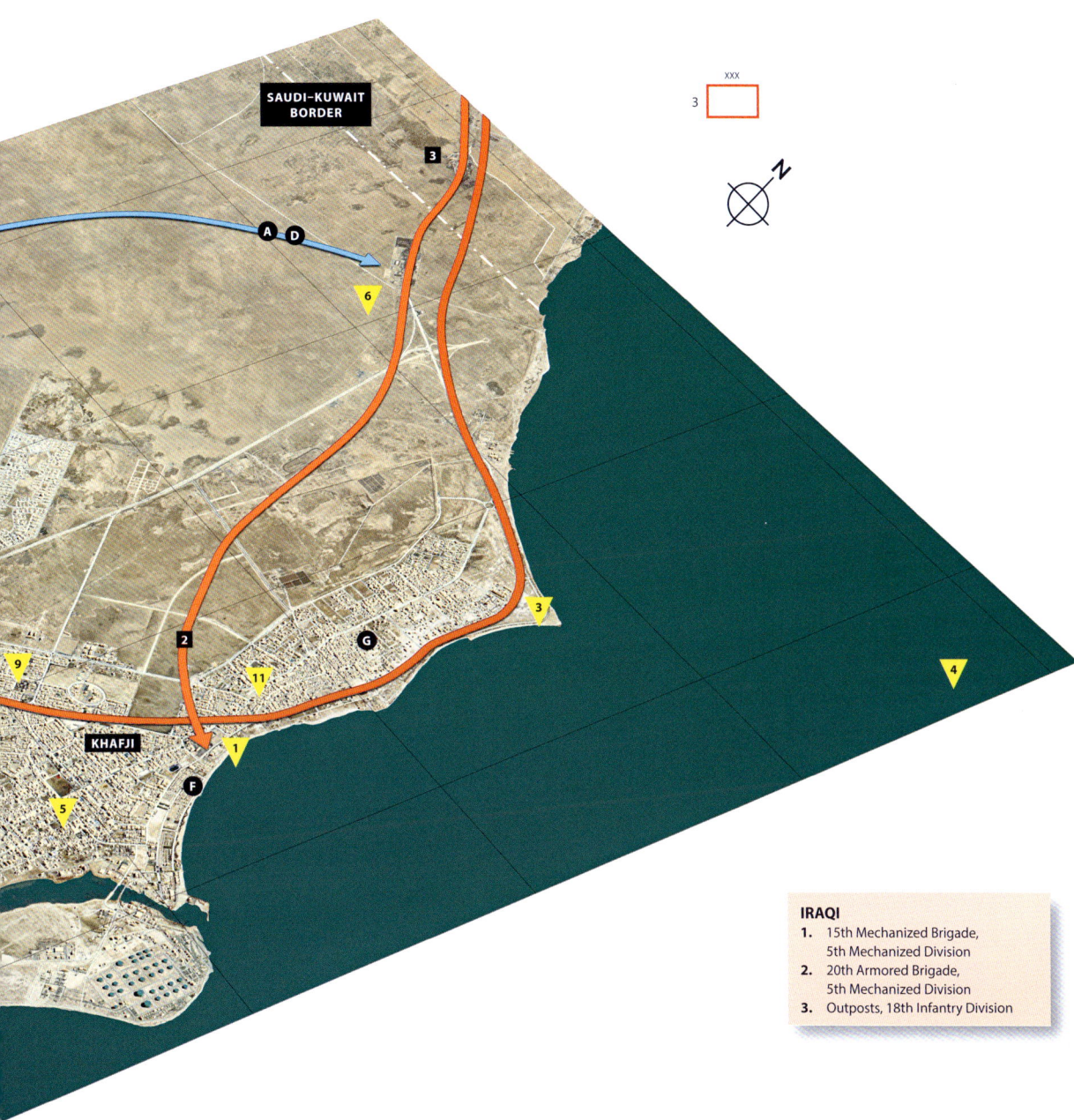

IRAQI
1. 15th Mechanized Brigade, 5th Mechanized Division
2. 20th Armored Brigade, 5th Mechanized Division
3. Outposts, 18th Infantry Division

EVENTS

1. At 2015hrs on January 29, the 20th Armored Brigade of the Iraqi 5th Mechanized Division crosses the undefended Saudi–Kuwait border and takes up defensive positions near the desalinization plant outside the town.

2. In the wake of the 20th Armored Brigade, the reinforced 15th Mechanized Brigade reaches the southern end of Khafji around 2315hrs.

3. Iraqi columns are strafed by AC-130 gunships and AH-1 attack helicopters, but it is not enough to blunt the attack.

4. A subsidiary seaborne raid by the Iraqi Navy's Brigade 440 in 15 small boats is intercepted by US Navy and Royal Navy aircraft and helicopters, and the attack foiled before they reach their destination.

5. Small observation teams from Company A, Marine 3rd Reconnaissance Battalion remain in Khafji and report on the situation by radio.

6. On the morning of January 30, the 5th Battalion, 2nd SANG Brigade along with a company of M60A1 tanks of the 8th MODA Tank Brigade move northeast to block the coastal road to prevent further Iraqi reinforcements in Khafji.

7. Around 1800hrs on January 30, 7th Battalion, 2nd SANG Brigade, supported by two companies of Qatari AMX-30 tanks, stage the first attack against the Iraqi positions in Khafji. The Saudi troops take heavy losses.

8. Qatari AMX-30 tanks engage in a firefight with Iraqi T-55 tanks along the southern outskirts of the city.

9. Coalition air strikes and artillery barrages continue against Iraqi positions in Khafji through January 30.

10. On the afternoon of January 31, the 7th Battalion is reinforced by the 8th Battalion, 2nd SANG Brigade that succeeds in pushing into the city.

11. With their defenses crumbling, the two Iraqi brigades of the 5th Mechanized Division are ordered to retreat from Khafji at 1800hrs on January 31.

12. Saudi troops regain control of Khafji on February 1. The Iraqis lost 112 tanks and AFVs, 74 other vehicles, and 20 artillery pieces, and suffered 66 killed, 137 wounded, and 566 missing.

THE BATTLE OF KHAFJI, JANUARY 31, 1991 (PP. 54–55)

In response to the Iraqi capture of Ras al-Khafji on the night of January 29/30, Lt. Col. Matar, commander of the 7th Combined Arms Battalion of the Saudi Arabian National Guard's 2nd King Abdulaziz Brigade, was ordered to advance on the city. The original message at 1600hrs instructed Matar to screen the southern side of the city. By the time the battalion arrived south of Khafji, the instructions had been expanded to include the capture of the city. Riyadh provided no information on the size of the Iraqi force, and the Saudis presumed it was only a reinforced company or understrength battalion when in fact it was two brigades. Lt. Col. Matar organized the attack with two mounted companies forward and a third in reserve. The attack was supported by two companies of AMX-30 tanks of the Qatari Brigade. The Saudi attack began an hour before midnight and was met by intense Iraqi fire that an accompanying US adviser described as "flabbergasting." The two sides exchanged fire for two hours and, at 0320hrs, the 7th Battalion withdrew to a neighboring Saudi National Guard barracks nearby. The brigade subsequently ordered the 6th and 8th Battalions to attach one company each to the 7th Battalion and the attack resumed at 0830hrs on February 1. Seen here are two different types of V-150 armored vehicle, the one at the left **(1)** armed with a 90mm Cockerill gun and the one at the right **(2)** with a 20mm Oerlikon autocannon as they passed the gateway arch **(3)** on the southwestern side of the city. The reinforced 7th Battalion made good progress, and at 1000hrs, the remainder of the 8th Battalion joined the fight while the 5th Battalion staged an attack to the north of Khafji to cut the road to the Kuwait border. Khafji was finally recaptured on February 1. The SANG attacks were supported by US Marine attack helicopters **(4)**.

The 2nd SANG Brigade involved in the fighting at Khafji was equipped with the Cadillac-Gage V-150S armored personnel carrier as seen here. The vehicle to the left is a Pinzgauer Turbo D light truck obtained from the Austrian Steyr-Puch company.

to block the road, while the 7-2nd SANG Brigade and the Qatari Brigade approached Khafji from the southwest. The first tank skirmishes began around 1800hrs when Qatari AMX-30 tanks engaged several T-55 tanks in the outskirts of the town.

The Saudi 7th Battalion, 2nd SANG Brigade was mounted on Cadillac-Gage V-150 wheeled APCs and made a charge directly into the town. After intense close-quarter fighting, the battered 7th Battalion was withdrawn to recuperate on the afternoon of January 31. The effort shifted to the 8th Battalion, 2nd SANG Brigade, which resumed the attack. Coalition artillery and air attacks intensified through the day. The Iraqi 5th Mechanized Division was granted permission to withdraw and ordered the retreat at 1800hrs on the night of January 31. Khafji was captured by the SANG on February 1, with clean-up operations around the town for a few days. The Iraqis lost 112 tanks and AFVs, 74 other vehicles, and 20 artillery pieces, and suffered 66 killed, 137 wounded, and 566 missing. JFC-East lost ten Saudi V-150 AFVs and two Qatari AMX-30 tanks.

A pair of V-150S armored vehicles of the 2nd SANG Brigade move through Khafji on February 1, 1991, after the recapture of the city. The lead vehicle is the variant armed with a 90mm Cockerill gun, while behind it is the armored personnel carrier version. (Georges Merillon, Getty Images)

The Iraqis regarded the Khafji raid as a victory, since it "proved that the Iraqi forces were highly trained since they managed to launch a well-planned and successful night attack despite the enemy's spy satellites, drones, surveillance aircraft and technical superiority." According to the divisional commander, the morale of the troops in the unit soared afterwards despite the losses.

The Coalition perspective of the Khafji battles was very different. Many army assessments of the Iraqi Army prior to Khafji depicted the Iraqi Army as a well-equipped, battle-hardened, determined foe. Khafji and the associated raids led to a reevaluation. A later assessment concluded that, "Khafji showed [the Iraqis] as incapable at this stage of the war of mounting an operational maneuver involving multiple divisions." The US Marine Corps in particular thought that the Khafji raid had seriously deflated the reputation of the Iraqi Army and gave the Marines greater confidence in their ability to defeat Iraqi forces in the upcoming ground campaign.

THE GROUND CAMPAIGN BEGINS: JOINT FORCES COMMAND AND THE I MEF

The Coalition began a number of operations along the frontier before the formal start of the ground campaign. In the days before "G-Day," the US 1st Cavalry Division staged a number of demonstrations near the Wadi al-Batin to convince the Iraqis that the riverbed would be a major avenue of Coalition advance and to distract the Iraqis from the actual buildup of VII Corps forces further west. Other units along the frontier sent patrols into the Saddam Line obstacles belts to determine the location of forward Iraqi positions. Artillery and helicopter strikes along the border increased in frequency.

The ground campaign began before dawn on G-Day, Sunday, February 24, 1991. The winter weather was rainy and overcast, with the cloud cover mixed with smoke from oil fires started by the Iraqi Army on February 22 in

An M9 ACE (armored combat earthmover) and an AAVP-7A1 amphibious assault vehicle of the 2nd Marine Division move towards the Kuwaiti border on February 24, 1991 to begin breaching operations against the Saddam Line.

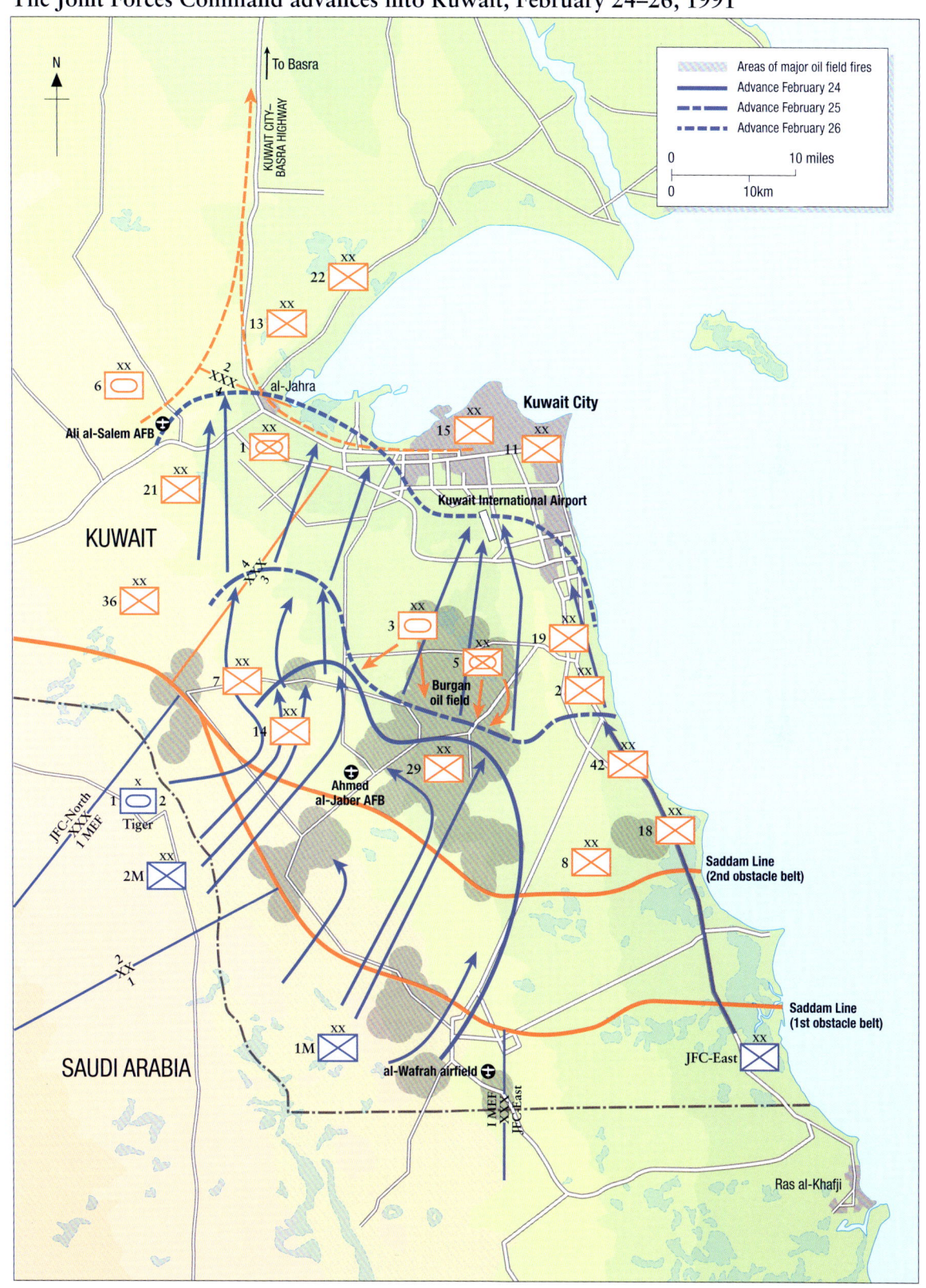
The Joint Forces Command advances into Kuwait, February 24–26, 1991

A Marine M198 155mm howitzer provides fire support for the 2nd Marine Division attack into Kuwait on February 24, 1991.

the hopes of obscuring the battlefield from Coalition air attack. The weather proved to be variable. On G-Day, the skies were overcast with rain until 1000hrs. Visibility was good at dawn but by late morning visibility fell to only 200m in many areas due to blowing sand and stronger winds.

Early on February 24, a chemical defense unit detected an unidentified agent in the air that led to orders for the I MEF to don their chemical protective battledress. No evidence of chemical weapons was ever found and the detection unit was probably confused by substances in the oil-fire smoke.

The I MEF was the primary assault element of the JFC, attacking the Iraqi 3 Corps. The plan expected the I MEF to lead the advance to Kuwait City but anticipated that Arab units from the adjoining JFC-East would liberate the city.

The right flank of the I MEF attack was led by the 1st Marine Division. The division's 1st Combat Engineer Battalion had been reinforced with specialized breaching equipment including tank-mounted mine plows,

A column from Task Force Breach Alpha, 2nd Marine Division is led by an M60A1 (RISE Passive Appliqué Armor) fitted with Track Width Mine Plough (TWMP) to assist in breaching the forward Iraqi minefields. It is followed by a column of AAVP-7A1 armored amphibious assault vehicles.

mine-clearing line charges, M9 ACE (armored combat earthmovers), and fascine bundles for the AAV-7A1 armored amphibian vehicles to fill antitank ditches. A steady stream of Iraqi deserters convinced the Marines that the forward Iraqi defenses of the 89th Brigade, 29th Infantry Division near the Kuwait border were on the verge of collapse. As a result, the 1st Marine Division decided to conduct an "infiltration" before the formal start of the ground offensive to begin the breaching process. At 1800hrs on February 23, combat engineers began clearing lanes to permit an early advance by Task Force (Task Force) Grizzly. This unit was based on the headquarters of the 4th Marines with two battalions from the 7th Marines reinforced with tanks and AAV-7A1s. The other breaching element was TF Taro based around the 3rd Marines. By midnight, both TF Grizzly and TF Taro had breached the initial Iraqi obstacle belt and moved to either side of the cleared lanes to serve as blocking forces for the subsequent wave.

The next wave of the 1st Marine Division was assigned to breach the second Iraqi obstacle belt located about 25km from the frontier. This force consisted of TF Ripper on the left flank, aiming for the Ahmed al-Jaber airbase, and TF Papa Bear on the right flank aiming towards the al-Burgan oil fields; TF Shepherd served as a screening force towards the northeast. TF Ripper was through the second obstacle belt by 1215hrs. The initial Iraqi response was weak, with most units either withdrawing or surrendering. A major hindrance was the sheer numbers of Iraqi prisoners. One of the few areas of active resistance was in the TF Papa Bear sector near the al-Burgan oil fields, defended by the Iraqi 22nd Brigade, 5th Mechanized Division. Team Ripper made its way out of the second obstacle belt and began its turn to the northwest towards al-Jaber airbase around 1630hrs. One of the few missions to go awry was the heliborne insertion of TF X-Ray, with the landing called off that evening due to its arrival after dark and the chaotic battlefield conditions. The 1st Marine Division captured or destroyed 600 tanks and 450 AFVs on the first day and took 10,365 prisoners.

The left flank of the I MEF attack was conducted by the 2nd Marine Division, reinforced by the Tiger Brigade (US Army 1st Brigade, 2nd Armored Division). The initial phase was similar to that of the 1st Marine Division

A US Marine Corps AAVP-7A1 of the I MEF advances into Kuwait on G-Day, February 24, 1991.

A pair of M109A1 155mm self-propelled howitzers of the Egyptian 188th Medium Range Artillery Brigade, 4th Armored Division. The Egyptian 4th Armored Division served with JFC-North in the western sector of Kuwait during the ground campaign.

to the southeast, with TF Breach Alpha conducting the initial penetration of the Saddam Line starting at 0600hrs. This reinforced combat engineer force consisted of 18 AAV-7A1, each with M154 three-shot mine-clearing line charges, two M60A1 dozer tanks, 16 M60A1 tanks with track-width mine plows towing an M59 line-charge trailer, four M60A1 tanks with mine rakes, six M1A1 tanks with mine plows, 22 AAVP-7A1 with engineer squads, 15 M9 ACE, and 39 M58 line-charge trailers. The cleared lanes were marked by engineers, and the task forces continued to grind through successive obstacle belts. The breaching units suffered the most casualties on G-Day, with the Marine 2nd Division suffering mine damage to seven M60A1 tanks, one M1A1 tank, and two AAV-7A1 amtracs. Resistance in the 2nd Marine Division sector was very weak, as was evident from the total of 14 casualties suffered on the first day.

The battleship USS *Wisconsin* (BB-64) fires a round from one of the Mk.7 16in/.50 cal guns against targets in Kuwait during the ground campaign. The US Navy battleships were used primarily to provide fire support for advancing Saudi units of JFC-East, directed by US Marine ANGLICO (Air Naval Gunfire Liaison Company) teams.

To the east of the I MEF, the Saudi-led JFC-East began its advance along the coastal highway towards Kuwait City while facing the Iraqi 18th Division. This advance was supported by two US battleships off the coast, with their fire directed by US Marine ANGLICO (Air Naval Gunfire Liaison Company) teams. To the west of the I MEF, the Egyptian 2 Corps was slowed down by one of the few active fire trenches and made little progress on G-Day.

The Iraqi 3 Corps commander, Maj. Gen. Salah Aboud, received a stream of reports from his units on February 24, many boasting about successful counter-attacks. By evening, the 3 Corps staff had prepared an ambitious plan to counter-attack the I MEF at al-Jaber airbase, based on the 7th Division and the remnants of the 5th Mechanized Division that had been chewed up during the Khafji battle. In conjunction with this attack, the 8th Infantry Division and 3rd Armored Division were expected to re-establish control over the Saddam Line from the al-Jaber airbase westward to the boundaries with the 4 Corps.

A Saudi Army column led by an M113A1 armored personnel carrier moves along a mine-cleared path on the Kuwait coast during the advance of the JFC-East force in late February 1991.

The Marines anticipated the Iraqi attack based on prisoner reports, captured maps, and Iraqi radio chatter. The Iraqi counter-attack materialized around dawn on February 25. At 0515hrs, TF Shepherd and TF Ripper of the 1st Marine Division engaged in an hour-long firefight with an Iraqi column emerging out of the gloom. Intelligence had identified several of the Iraqi units and both the 22nd Brigade, 5th Mechanized Division and 15th Brigade, 3rd Armored Division were pummeled by Marine artillery. Around 0800hrs, the remnants of the 22nd Brigade, 5th Mechanized Division appeared in front of the headquarters of TF Papa Bear. Bizarrely, the unit commander dismounted his tank, strode up to the Marine officers, and surrendered. The rest of the 22nd Brigade continued to fight, supported by a brigade from the 8th Infantry Division. The elements near the TF Papa Bear HQ were halted by Marines firing AT-4 antitank rockets. The Marine 1st Tank Battalion counter-attacked, knocking out at least 18 Iraqi armored vehicles. The remains of the 22nd Brigade were then attacked by AH-1 attack helicopters of the 3rd Marine Aircraft Wing. By the end of the skirmish, the Iraqis had lost 50 tanks and 25 other AFVs, and 300 Iraqi soldiers had surrendered. Another Iraqi column hit the 1st Marine Division headquarters but was beaten off by the HQ's security detachment. The Marines had planned to bypass the burning al-Burgan oil fields, assessing the area as uninhabitable due to the dense smoke. However, the Iraqi 15th Brigade, 3rd Armored Division moved through the oil fields and hit the 1st Battalion, 1st Marines in a skirmish lasting several hours. The Iraqi counter-attacks against the 1st Marine Division on February 25 are often called the Battle of Burgan.

The Iraqi counter-attack in the northwest against the 2nd Marine Division was much less extensive than the attacks against the 1st Marine Division. Dubbed the "Reveille Counter-attack," it was conducted by elements of the Iraqi 8th Division and 3rd Armored Division, starting around dawn. This fizzled out during the morning. By the afternoon, the Iraqi 3 Corps ordered a general withdrawal into Kuwait City. They reported to Baghdad that the 7th, 14th, and 29th Divisions were combat ineffective.

THE "GREAT WHEEL" BEGINS: XVIII AIRBORNE CORPS

The left flank of the Coalition forces was the XVIII Airborne Corps located in the open desert to the west of Kuwait. Its initial mission, the seizure of as-Salman airbase, was assigned to the French Division Daguet, reinforced by the 2nd Brigade, 82nd Airborne Division. This formation departed its start

A Marine LAV takes part in the capture of Kuwait International Airport on February 27, 1991.

line around 0100hrs on February 24. The French units swept past a number of outposts of the Iraqi 45th Division and captured the Iraqi division's main concentration about 50km into Iraq, along with about 2,500 Iraqi prisoners. The advance continued northward, leading to a clash between the division's AMX-30 tanks and a company of Iraqi T-55 tanks south of as-Salman. After an artillery preparation, Division Daguet and the 2nd Brigade conducted the

A Marine Light Armored Infantry Battalion equipped with the LAV-25 scout/reconnaissance vehicle in northern Kuwait at the end of the war.

The XVIII Airborne Corps and VII Corps, February 24–27, 1991

A pair of M1A1 Abrams tanks and an M2A1 Bradley at the al-Mutla police complex near al-Jahra at the end of the fighting. A destroyed Iraqi T-72 tank can be seen near the buildings.

main attack against the town and airbase, surrounding the area by 1800hrs. The two other brigades of the 82nd Airborne, mounted on trucks, followed up the main highway, clearing pockets of resistance that had been bypassed earlier in the day. This operation secured the Coalition's left flank and led to the control of one of the few significant highways west of Kuwait.

The 101st Airborne Division was assigned to conduct a deep heliborne mission to establish a forward operating base codenamed FOB Cobra 170km inside Iraq. Scheduled to begin at 0500hrs, the operation was delayed until 0705hrs due to fog. The first lift was provided by 66 UH-60 Blackhawk and 30 CH-47 Chinook helicopters, with escort from AH-1 Cobra and AH-64 Apache attack helicopters, taking about 40 minutes to reach their objective. Two further lifts were conducted to deliver the rest of the brigade.

The crews of the 72nd Engineering Company, 24th Infantry Division test a Full Width Mine Plough attached to an M728 CEV (combat engineer vehicle) on February 18, 1991, days prior to the start of Operation *Desert Storm*.

A Chinese-supplied Type 69-II tank of a tank regiment of the Iraqi 45th Infantry Division knocked out by the French Division Daguet during the fighting for the as-Salman airbase. The "boom-shields" on the turret were distinctive of the Chinese tanks supplied to Iraq as a method to protect against RPG-7 antitank rocket launchers.

Some 300 helicopters eventually took part in the mission, one of the largest heliborne operations in history. Once secure, FOB Cobra became the staging area for further airmobile operations into Iraq. Iraqi resistance in the area was minimal but poor weather was a significant threat to an operation that depended on helicopter support.

On February 25, the 3rd Brigade, 101st Airborne Division conducted the next phase of the operation, seizing control of Highway 8, the key lifeline from Baghdad to Basra, on the stretch running from as-Samawah to al-Nasiriyah along the Euphrates River. Around noon, 30 Chinooks carried three anti-armor companies along with their TOW missile-equipped HMMWVs to a spot 40km south of the Euphrates. They were followed by a mission at 1500hrs to deliver 500 troops directly along Highway 8 using UH-60 helicopters. Both elements joined each other the next day after the HMMWV force negotiated the rain-soaked desert.

The heavy element of the XVIII Corps was the 24th Infantry Division (Mech), assigned to secure the Euphrates River valley east of FOB Cobra. This division had 25,000 troops, 241 M1A1 tanks, 221 Bradleys, 6,500 wheeled and 1,300 tracked vehicles, and 94 helicopters. In advance, the 2nd Squadron, 4th Cavalry scouted the route, followed by the rest of the division at 1500hrs in an advance three brigades wide. The advance after dark in trackless desert was aided by technical innovations such as GPS navigation aids and "Budd lights," an antenna-mounted infrared light intended to help identify friendly forces and prevent friendly fire in the dark. The division encountered little resistance and reached 120km into Iraq by midnight. The right flank of the XVIII Airborne Corps advance was conducted by the 3rd Armored Cavalry Regiment. It proceeded to the east of the 24th Infantry Division.

The advance by the 24th Infantry Division on February 25 was complicated more by terrain than Iraqi resistance. The division had advanced along the eastern edge of the Sahra al-Hajarah (Desert of Stone) plateau on the first phase. On reaching about 60km south of the Euphrates, the terrain began to descend into a broken terrain of wadis and sabkhas, the latter of which had turned into muddy sandflats due to the winter rain.

A pair of French AMX-30B2 tanks of the 4e Règiment de Dragons, Division Daguet following the fighting for as-Salman airbase.

This area had been labeled "the great dismal bog" in prewar planning and the 2-4th Cavalry spent the night of February 25 finding passable routes through the area. The division's brigades made their way to the vicinity of the Euphrates on February 26, with the 197th Brigade assigned to a position near Tallil airbase, the 2nd Brigade near Jalibah airbase, and the 1st Brigade to the north on Highway 8. The afternoon of February 26 saw the first serious Iraqi resistance when facing the 47th and 49th Infantry Divisions.

THE GREAT WHEEL'S HEAVY METAL: VII CORPS

In the days preceding G-Day, the American units along the Iraqi border conducted probes and engaged in cross-border artillery preparations. These actions were vigorous enough that Iraqi official histories consider February 21 to have been the start of the ground campaign. The original plan had been to start the VII Corps offensive on G+1, February 25, but the speedy progress of the neighboring XVIII Corps led to the decision to start 14 hours early. The weather was "more like Germany than Arabia" in the words of one American tanker – cold, windy, rainy, and overcast.

The spearhead for the VII Corps advance was the 2nd Armored Cavalry Regiment (ACR) whose mission was to probe the Iraqi defenses to locate the RGFC main force. The 2nd ACR was positioned on a front 40km wide. Around 1430hrs, it moved forward with a screen of Bradleys and AH-1 Cobra attack helicopters. About 10km behind were the regiment's M1A1 Abrams tanks and the remainder of their Bradleys. Within two hours, the 2nd ACR advanced 40km, accumulating a growing number of Iraqi prisoners from the Iraqi 26th Infantry Division. Contact with the Iraqi Army was light, with some scattered engagements against T-55 tanks and BMP infantry fighting vehicles.

Following behind the 2nd ACR were two heavy maneuver divisions, the 1st Armored Division on the left and the 3rd Armored Division on the right. In open desert terrain, the divisional formations were enormous, some 15km wide and 45km deep, screened by the divisional cavalry squadrons.

A pair of M1A1 Abrams tanks of the 3rd Armored Division during the VII Corps advance into the Iraqi desert in late February 1991. In the upper right is a Bradley fighting vehicle, while a column of support vehicles can be seen on the horizon.

There was little contact with the Iraqi Army on the first day, evident from the small bag of prisoners – only 1,300 in all of VII Corps. This was in no small measure due to the paucity of Iraqi defenses in the desert west of Kuwait.

Closer to Kuwait, the other two divisions moved more slowly in order to synchronize their advance with the "Great Wheel" plan. The 1st Infantry Division began the day by seizing the security zones in front of the Iraqi 26th and 48th Infantry Divisions, starting around 0530hrs. By 0915hrs, the Iraqi forward defenses had been overcome and breaching operations

A burning Iraqi 9P122 missile-armed tank destroyer is passed by an FV-432 Mk.2 armored personnel carrier of the Royal Scots Dragoon Guards, UK 1st Armoured Division during the fighting in Kuwait on February 28, 1991.

A Type 69-II tank of the Iraqi 52nd Armored Division burns after having been hit by a British Challenger tank of the UK 1st Armoured Division during the fighting west of the Wadi al-Batin on February 28, 1991.

continued. After a 30-minute artillery preparation, the main attack occurred at 1500hrs. The original plan had anticipated that it would take 18 hours to break through the Iraqi defenses, but it in fact took two hours. The breaching operation was wide since it also cleared a sector for the British 1st Armoured Division. The British division was the VII Corps formation closest to the Kuwaiti border and the Wadi al-Batin, and so was the hinge for the "Great Wheel" maneuver. The 1st Cavalry Division was also in this sector, serving as the corps reserve. Its other mission was to serve as a prod to accelerate the progress of JFC-North if the Arab units failed to advance sufficiently on the Kuwaiti side of the border.

On G+1, the left flank of VII Corps began to run into more substantial Iraqi defenses. The 1st Armored Division advanced through the defense perimeter of the Iraqi 26th Infantry Division. As elements of the division were encountered, they were subjected to artillery and helicopter attack, usually resulting in mass surrenders. The divisional tank regiment resisted but was bludgeoned by gunfire from M1A1 Abrams tanks, losing about 50 tanks and AFVs in a short firefight. By early afternoon, the 1st Armored Division began approaching its objective of al-Busayyah. Due to the day's unimpeded progress, the 2nd ACR and 3rd Armored Division began the turn eastward towards Kuwait and the RGFC, starting the "Great Wheel" maneuver.

The British 1st Armoured Division began moving through the mine breach at noon on G+1, heading towards a confrontation with the Iraqi 52nd Armored Division. The neighboring 1st Infantry Division began its advance into Iraq. The division captured two brigade headquarters as well as the divisional headquarters of the Iraqi 26th Division along with its staff.

The British flag waves above a Warrior infantry fighting vehicle of the Royal Scots Dragoon Guards, 1st Armoured Division as it advances past a destroyed Iraqi column along the Basra–Kuwait City Highway near Kuwait City following the retreat of Iraqi forces on February 28, 1991.

THE WITHDRAWAL ORDER

By G+1, February 25, Saddam and the senior command in Baghdad had come to realize that the Iraqi Army in Kuwait was being overwhelmed more quickly than anticipated. The situation west of the Wadi al-Batin still was not clear to senior commanders in Baghdad. Saddam hastily made the monumental decision to change the strategic goal from defense of Kuwait to the survival of the Iraqi Army.

Saddam instructed the army chief of staff to prepare a withdrawal plan to extract the Iraqi Army out of Kuwait and back towards the Basra area in Iraq. The Iraqi corps were instructed to prepare for movement on the night of February 25/26. Priority was given to the units that were most threatened by the advance of the I MEF: 3 Corps, the Gulf Operations command, and the Popular Forces and state workers in Kuwait City. The second wave of withdrawals was to include the 4 Corps in western Kuwait, the 7 Corps in the desert west of Kuwait, and the 2 Corps on the coast in northeastern Kuwait. The RGFC Corps and Jihad Corps were instructed to remain in position as long as possible to shield the withdrawals. The intention was to create a new series of echeloned defenses emanating from Basra.

The corps headquarters were informed of the withdrawal order by radio, but Baghdad sent officers by road with more detailed instructions to make certain that the directive was understood. The withdrawal orders created chaos in Kuwait. There had been no previous planning for a withdrawal, and the hasty scheme drawn up on the afternoon of February 25 could not begin to provide adequate routes for the retreat of so many units in such a short period of time without leading to inevitable traffic jams. Furthermore,

The withdrawal order late on February 26 led to a precipitous retreat from Kuwait City along the highway to Basra. This became known as the "Highway of Death," as the trapped columns of vehicles were struck by Coalition air power.

there was widespread looting by Iraqi troops, particularly of Kuwaiti civilian vehicles.

Delays in conveying the withdrawal orders to the Gulf Operations Command in Kuwait City led to a last-minute and confused retreat from the city on G+2, February 26. The roads out of the city were clogged with a mixture of Iraqi troops and Iraqi bureaucrats who had overseen the occupation of Kuwait. Not all of the combat units of 3 Corps received the orders, so some units remained in place while the majority of the units fled. The withdrawal in 3 Corps was also confused since the previous corps orders had been to withdraw into Kuwait City for a final defense, while the second withdrawal order from Baghdad called for a withdrawal all the way north to the Basra area.

Early on G+3, February 26, the all-seeing eye of the E-8A JSTARS aircraft picked up the traffic fleeing from Kuwait City towards Baghdad. The I MEF's aviation element was the 3rd Marine Air Wing (MAW). The 3rd MAW had been attempting to provide close-air support to the I MEF near Kuwait International Airport and Mutla ridge that day, but there was too much smoke and cloud cover. As it happened, the area over Highway 80, the Kuwait City–Basra road, was relatively clear and choked full of targets. Marine A-6 Intruders struck the front and rear of the column with Mk.20 Rockeye II cluster bombs, starting an enormous traffic jam. Other Coalition aircraft joined the attack, eventually destroying or immobilizing 1,400–2,000 vehicles. The road was later dubbed the "Highway of Death" by journalists. Although there were lurid press accounts of thousands of Iraqi dead, troops who visited the area noted that the Iraqi soldiers took the first opportunity to evade the air attacks and escape on foot away from the road.

The I MEF first encountered the consequences of the withdrawal order outside of Kuwait City. The 1st Marine Division headed to the northeast towards Kuwait International Airport, while the 2nd Marine Division and the Tiger Brigade headed directly north to cut off the Iraqi retreat routes. The Tiger Brigade aimed for the town of al-Jahra, which was astride the

The Kuwait City–Basra road was littered with military as well as civilian vehicles. The T-62 tank seen here was from the 1st Tank Regiment, 6th Armored Brigade, 3rd "Saladin" Armored Division, and in the foreground is an MT-LB armored transporter.

two multi-lane highways in the area. In addition, the town was located on a terrain feature called the Mutla ridge. While the ridge was only about 7m (25ft) high, in the flat desert terrain the elevated ground offered a vista over the surrounding landscape. The brigade encountered numerous T-55 tanks, a significant bunker complex, and other Iraqi defenses, leading to a three-hour battle through the early evening. Once the dust had settled, the Tiger Brigade peered down to a scene of utter devastation on Highway 80 that had been attacked relentlessly by aircraft earlier in the day. Col. John Sylvester, commander of the Tiger Brigade, later described the scene on Highway 80:

> Vehicles kept coming into it, and it became like a stopped-up sink. Things kept piling up and piling up and piling up. Ultimately there were literally thousands of vehicles in there, fully half of which were enemy combat vehicles and half of which were looted and stolen. Everything from school buses, to ambulances, to brand new automobiles. Every single vehicle was stuffed with the loot of the city. Jewelry and furniture and clothes and people's personal belongings, and you name it. It was in there. Along with, in every vehicle that I saw, military paraphernalia. And all the vehicles were hot-wired. Even the ambulances were full of loot and booty. And it was very obvious that what had been stopped was the literal theft of the city.

By the time the I MEF had reached the outskirts of Kuwait City, they had knocked out or captured 1,040 Iraqi tanks, 608 armored personnel carriers, and 432 artillery pieces, and captured at least 20,000 prisoners.

BATTLES WITH THE REPUBLICAN GUARD

Although the first echelon of Iraqi defenses collapsed due to Saddam's withdrawal order, Baghdad had instructed the second echelon tactical reserve and the Republican Guard strategic reserve to shield the withdrawal. During the evening of February 25, three RGFC heavy divisions began to reorient themselves to counter the approaching VII Corps.

The Tawakalna RGFC Mechanized Division deployed in a defensive blocking position on the western Kuwaiti border. It took up positions to the west of the 12th Armored Division of the Jihad Corps, intermixed with elements of the division's 46th Armored Brigade. To the south of the Tawakalna Division was the remainder of the 12th Armored Division, consisting of the 37th Armored Brigade and 50th Mechanized Brigade. The 10th Armored Division of the Jihad Corps was behind it to its east. The Medina and Hammurabi RGFC armored divisions were placed north of these formations on either side of the Rumaylah oil fields.

The movement by the Republican Guard was spotted by the JSTARS surveillance aircraft in spite of the poor weather. This data helped shape the tactics of the oncoming VII Corps. As a result, the largest battles of the Gulf War took place on February 26–27 as Coalition forces began to collide with the Iraqi armored forces in the deserts west of Kuwait.

The first of these big tank battles started on February 26 when the 2nd ACR ran into isolated outposts of the 12th Armored Division, encountering numerous T-55 tanks and MT-LB armored transporters. By mid-afternoon, the intensity of the fighting increased, and the VII Corps was convinced that it had finally entered combat with the RGFC. Shortly after, the advancing US units ran into the outer security screen of the Tawakalna RGFC Division. Instead of T-55 tanks and MT-LB AFVs, the 2nd ACR and the neighboring 3rd Armored Division began encountering companies of dug-in T-72 tanks and BMP-1 infantry fighting vehicles, the better type of equipment associated with the RGFC units.

In the late afternoon of February 26, the 2nd ACR encountered the defensive positions of the 9th Armored Brigade and 18th Mechanized Brigade on the Tawakalna's left flank to the west of the IPSA (Iraqi Pipeline in Saudi Arabia) pipeline along the 60 Easting (Easting is a GPS coordinate corresponding to a longitude). At the time, the three armored squadrons of the 2nd ACR were serving as the spearhead of the VII Corps in front of the 1st Infantry Division, advancing on a front about 15 miles (20km) wide. The northernmost of these squadrons, the 2-2nd ACR, advanced unseen through the rain and mist, and initially was not spotted by the Iraqi troops. This began one of the most famous tank versus tank battles of the Gulf War. Many Iraqi Republican Guard troops were still in their dugouts away from their vehicles, not anticipating the arrival of American tanks so soon.

The 2-2nd ACR began engaging scattered tanks and BMPs of the 9th RGFC Armored Brigade along the 68 Easting. By dusk, the 2-2nd ACR entered the main defensive belt of the Republic Guard armored battalion near 73 Easting, coming under fire from a company of Iraqi T-72 tanks. However, the Iraqis could not get accurate ranges on the approaching American tanks due to the poor weather conditions, while the M1A1 Abrams tanks were able to use their thermal imaging sights to accurately locate and engage the Iraqi tanks. The engagements took place at a range of about 2,100m and most of the Iraqi tank projectiles fell far short of their intended targets. In a short engagement, 18 M1A1 tanks and 24 M3A1 Bradleys destroyed more than 30 dug-in T-72 tanks and 12 BMP-1s at no loss to themselves. A captured Iraqi mechanized infantry battalion commander said that he had started the fight with 900 soldiers, a few dozen BMP-1s, and an attached battalion of 36 T-72 tanks; when he was captured, all that survived were the 40 soldiers with him. A stunned Tawakalna tank battalion commander added that, "When the air campaign started, I had 39 [T-72] tanks. After 38 days of the air battle, I had 32 tanks. After 20 minutes against [the 2nd ACR], I had zero tanks." After dark, Apache helicopters struck the second tactical echelon of these brigades, causing heavy losses to three emplaced battalions. The 2nd ACR largely destroyed two Iraqi Republican Guard regiments.

With its mission of locating and fixing the Tawakalna Division accomplished, the 2nd ACR hunkered down along the 73 Easting, awaiting the arrival of the 1st Infantry Division. In a complicated and dangerous maneuver, the 1st Infantry Division passed through the 2nd ACR in the dark before midnight, to continue the battle with the Tawakalna Division. Its objective was codenamed Norfolk, located along the IPSA pipeline to the immediate west of the Iraq–Kuwait border. The 1st Infantry Division destroyed over 100 Iraqi armored vehicles of the 18th RGFC and 37th Brigades in a series of engagements on the night of February 26/27, reaching Objective Norfolk around dawn. The actions of the 2nd ACR and 1st Infantry Division largely destroyed two of the brigades of the Tawakalna RGFC Division in less than 12 hours of combat.

A pair of Bradleys of the 2nd ACR inspect a destroyed T-72 tank of the RGFC Tawakalna Division following the fighting on February 27, 1991.

To the north, the US 3rd Armored Division engaged the right flank of the Tawakalna Division. This battle pitted eight Iraqi tank and mechanized battalions totaling 122 tanks and 78 BMPs against ten US heavy tank/mechanized infantry battalions. The American attack began with concentrated air attacks from A-10 and F-16 aircraft, as well as one hour of concentrated gunfire from AC-130 Spectre gunships. The 3rd Armored Division initially encountered a tank regiment of the 9th Armored Brigade of the Tawakalna Division, with the fighting starting around 1630hrs. The Iraqi regiment put up a very spirited defense of its positions, holding the 1st Brigade, 3rd Armored Division at bay for most of the night. The neighboring 2nd Brigade, 3rd Armored Division made better progress, crunching through the 29th RGFC Mechanized Brigade towards Objective Dorset to the east. That night, a mechanized force from the Iraqi 29th Mechanized Brigade attempted to conduct a counter-attack but was ambushed by M1A1 Abrams tanks after dawn on February 27. This led to the prompt destruction of 17 T-72 tanks and 25 other armored vehicles.

In contrast to the Iraqi Army divisions encountered by the VII Corps along the frontier, the Tawakalna RGFC Division fought aggressively. It was defeated by the superior training of the US Army, which also enjoyed some significant technical advantages, notably the thermal imaging sights that proved invaluable on a battlefield obscured by rain, dust, and dark.

On the VII Corps left flank, two brigades of the 1st Armored Division intended to confront the RGFC Medina Armored Division on the outskirts of the Rumaylah oil fields. The Medina Division had been assigned to block the advance of the VII Corps towards Basra. An AH-1 Cobra helicopter from the division's 1-1st Cavalry spotted a battalion of the 29th Mechanized Brigade of the Tawakalna Division and a column of about 50 T-72 tanks. These were engaged by A-10 aircraft followed by rockets from the division's MLRS multiple rocket launchers. The tank fighting began after dark when the 3rd Brigade's TF 1-37th Armor crested a ridge and encountered an Iraqi regiment in reverse slope defense. The close-range night battle was complicated by Iraqi minefields, and at least four Abrams tanks were hit by T-72 tanks and BMPs that had been bypassed in the dark. After a night of intense fighting, the northern elements of the Tawakalna RGFC Division had lost a further 76 T-72 tanks, 84 BMPs, and numerous other vehicles and weapons.

THE REPUBLICAN GUARD CONFRONTS THE VII CORPS, NIGHT OF FEBRUARY 26–27, 1991

The "Great Wheel" triggers the largest tank battles of Operation *Desert Storm*.

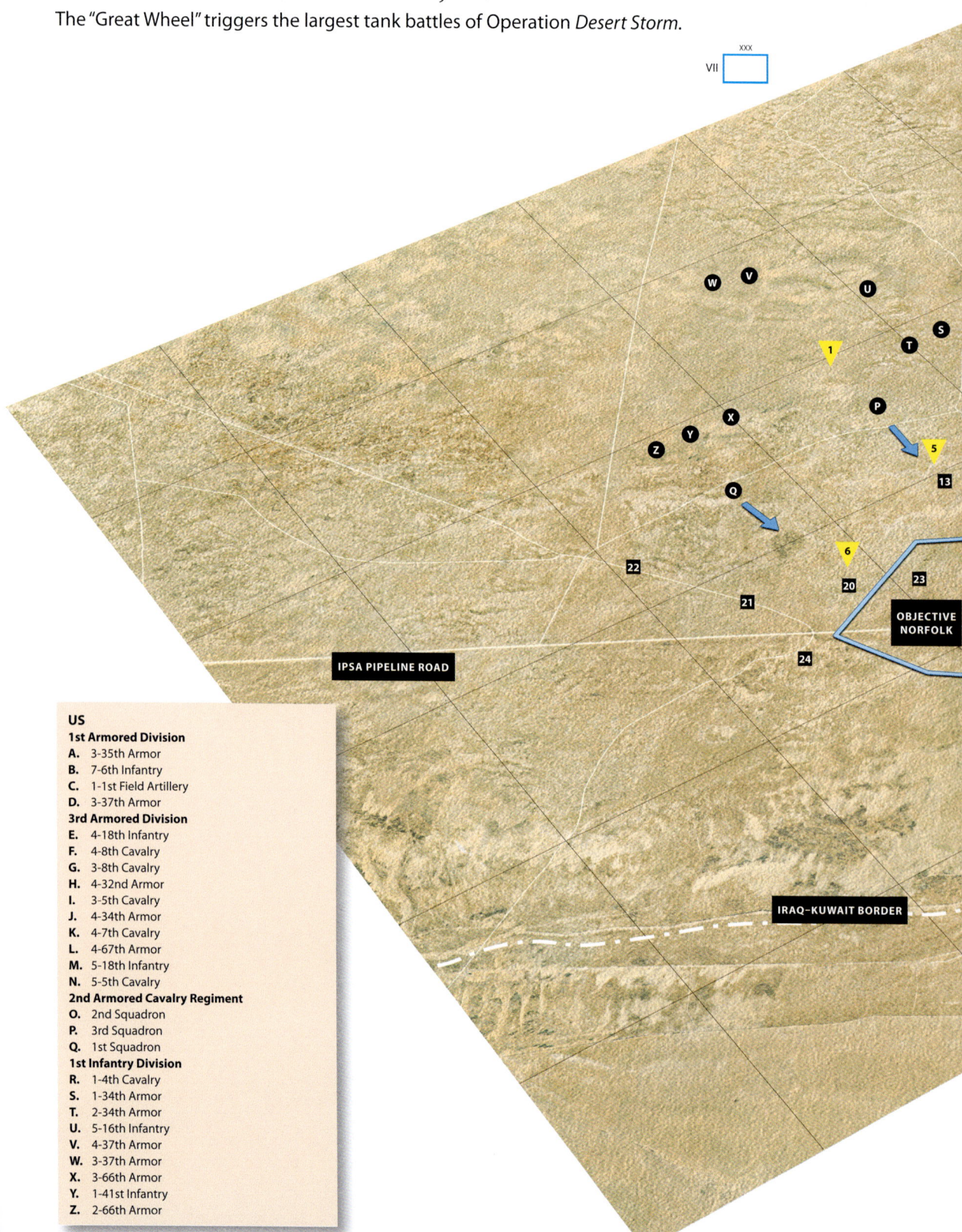

US
1st Armored Division
A. 3-35th Armor
B. 7-6th Infantry
C. 1-1st Field Artillery
D. 3-37th Armor
3rd Armored Division
E. 4-18th Infantry
F. 4-8th Cavalry
G. 3-8th Cavalry
H. 4-32nd Armor
I. 3-5th Cavalry
J. 4-34th Armor
K. 4-7th Cavalry
L. 4-67th Armor
M. 5-18th Infantry
N. 5-5th Cavalry
2nd Armored Cavalry Regiment
O. 2nd Squadron
P. 3rd Squadron
Q. 1st Squadron
1st Infantry Division
R. 1-4th Cavalry
S. 1-34th Armor
T. 2-34th Armor
U. 5-16th Infantry
V. 4-37th Armor
W. 3-37th Armor
X. 3-66th Armor
Y. 1-41st Infantry
Z. 2-66th Armor

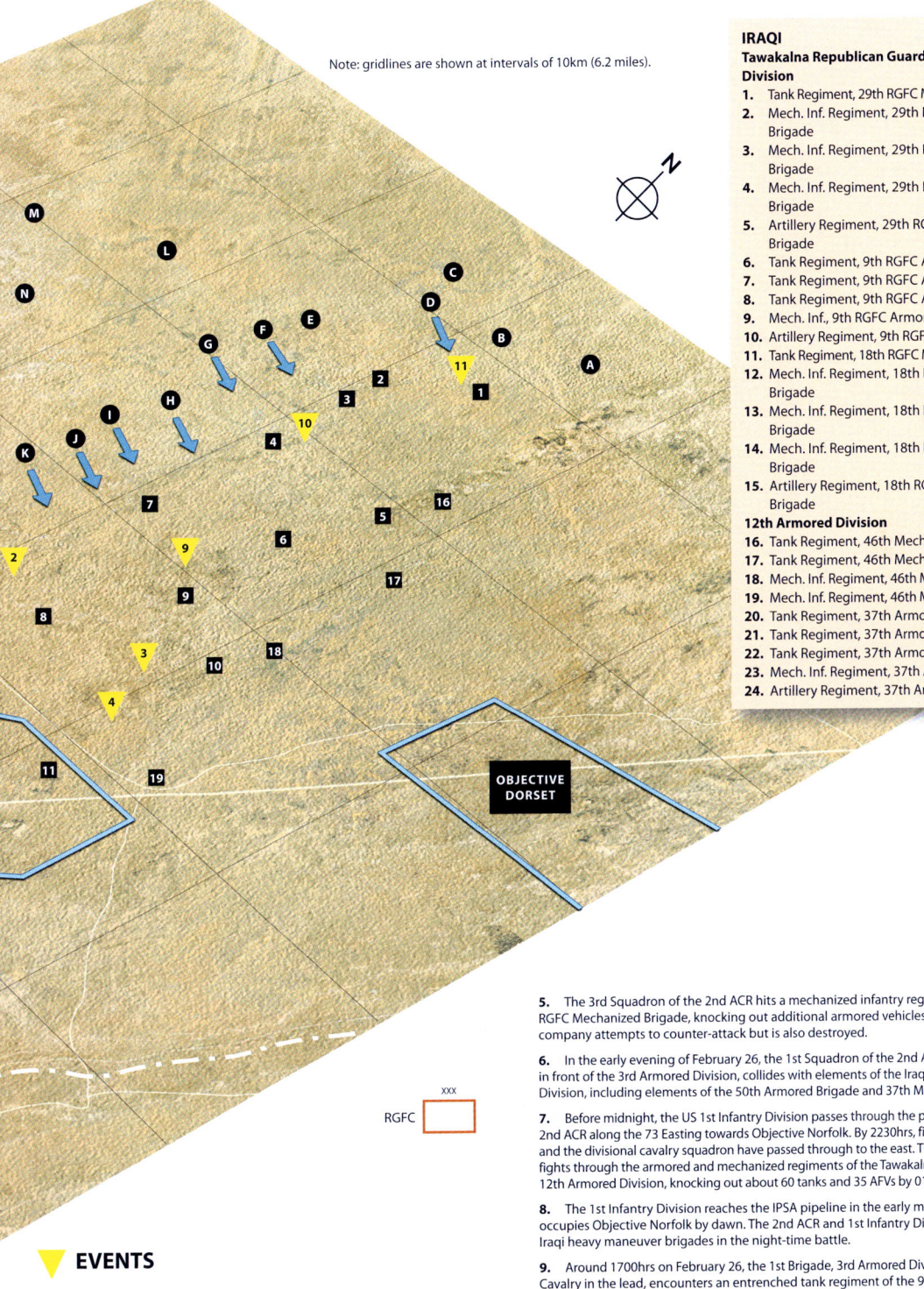

IRAQI

Tawakalna Republican Guard Mechanized Division

1. Tank Regiment, 29th RGFC Mechanized Brigade
2. Mech. Inf. Regiment, 29th RGFC Mechanized Brigade
3. Mech. Inf. Regiment, 29th RGFC Mechanized Brigade
4. Mech. Inf. Regiment, 29th RGFC Mechanized Brigade
5. Artillery Regiment, 29th RGFC Mechanized Brigade
6. Tank Regiment, 9th RGFC Armored Brigade
7. Tank Regiment, 9th RGFC Armored Brigade
8. Tank Regiment, 9th RGFC Armored Brigade
9. Mech. Inf., 9th RGFC Armored Brigade
10. Artillery Regiment, 9th RGFC Armored Brigade
11. Tank Regiment, 18th RGFC Mechanized Brigade
12. Mech. Inf. Regiment, 18th RGFC Mechanized Brigade
13. Mech. Inf. Regiment, 18th RGFC Mechanized Brigade
14. Mech. Inf. Regiment, 18th RGFC Mechanized Brigade
15. Artillery Regiment, 18th RGFC Mechanized Brigade

12th Armored Division

16. Tank Regiment, 46th Mechanized Brigade
17. Tank Regiment, 46th Mechanized Brigade
18. Mech. Inf. Regiment, 46th Mechanized Brigade
19. Mech. Inf. Regiment, 46th Mechanized Brigade
20. Tank Regiment, 37th Armored Brigade
21. Tank Regiment, 37th Armored Brigade
22. Tank Regiment, 37th Armored Brigade
23. Mech. Inf. Regiment, 37th Armored Brigade
24. Artillery Regiment, 37th Armored Brigade

▼ EVENTS

1. Around 1500hrs, February 26, the 2nd Armored Cavalry Regiment, in the vanguard of the VII Corps, passes eastward over Phase Line Tangerine on the 60 Easting GPS coordinate. The regiment is arrayed into three component armored squadrons forward of the advancing 3rd Armored Division and 1st Infantry Division.

2. Around 1530hrs on February 26, 2-2nd ACR, the northernmost of the squadrons, encounters a forward outpost of Iraqi tanks and BMPs of the 9th RGFC Armored Brigade along the 68 Easting and begins engaging them.

3. Around 1620hrs, Eagle Troop and Ghost Troop of the 2-2nd ACR surprise a tank regiment of the 9th RGFC Brigade near 73 Easting and overwhelm it.

4. From 1700hrs to 2010hrs, elements of Iraqi 9th RGFC Armored Brigade launch small counter-attacks against 2-2nd ACR along the 73 Easting.

5. The 3rd Squadron of the 2nd ACR hits a mechanized infantry regiment of the 18th RGFC Mechanized Brigade, knocking out additional armored vehicles. An Iraqi T-72 tank company attempts to counter-attack but is also destroyed.

6. In the early evening of February 26, the 1st Squadron of the 2nd ACR, operating in front of the 3rd Armored Division, collides with elements of the Iraqi 12th Armored Division, including elements of the 50th Armored Brigade and 37th Mechanized Brigade.

7. Before midnight, the US 1st Infantry Division passes through the positions of the 2nd ACR along the 73 Easting towards Objective Norfolk. By 2230hrs, five heavy battalions and the divisional cavalry squadron have passed through to the east. The "Big Red One" fights through the armored and mechanized regiments of the Tawakalna Division and 12th Armored Division, knocking out about 60 tanks and 35 AFVs by 0100hrs February 27.

8. The 1st Infantry Division reaches the IPSA pipeline in the early morning hours and occupies Objective Norfolk by dawn. The 2nd ACR and 1st Infantry Division destroy four Iraqi heavy maneuver brigades in the night-time battle.

9. Around 1700hrs on February 26, the 1st Brigade, 3rd Armored Division, with TF 3-5th Cavalry in the lead, encounters an entrenched tank regiment of the 9th RGFC Armored Brigade of the Tawakalna Division. The 1st Brigade engages the strongpoint through the night, with the 4-32nd Armor along the northern perimeter of the strongpoint and the 4-34th Armor along its southern edge.

10. At 2200hrs on February 26, the 2nd Brigade, 3rd Armored Division begins to systematically breach the defenses of the 29th RGFC Mechanized Brigade, Tawakalna Division. By 0200hrs on February 28, the brigade has pushed to the 73 Easting through the first belt of Iraqi defenses.

11. Before midnight on February 26, the 3rd Brigade of the 1st Armored Division begins an attack against the northernmost tank regiment of the Tawakalna Division near the 68 Easting. The fighting leads to the destruction of 24 T-72 tanks and 14 BMPs. However, the division's main mission is the Medina RGFC Division, an engagement that takes place later on February 28.

By February 27, the VII Corps had five heavy maneuver divisions moving towards Kuwait after the 1st Cavalry Division was taken from the reserve and directed to the left flank of the VII Corps advance. The VII Corps front-line on this day from left to right consisted of the 1st Armored Division, 3rd Armored Division, 1st Infantry Division, 2nd ACR, and British 1st Armoured Division. This force included over 1,500 tanks, 1,500 other armored infantry vehicles, 650 artillery pieces, and thousands of other vehicles moving en masse eastward towards Basra and Kuwait. This resulted in a series of disjointed encounters as the VII Corps divisions struck the Republican Guard units as well as second-echelon Iraqi armored divisions of the Jihad Corps. The Republican Guard divisions in most cases consisted of separate brigade defense strongholds, with the tanks, BMPs, and APCs entrenched in fixed defensive positions.

A brigade of the RGFC Adnan Mechanized Division attempted to intervene in the fighting west of the Kuwaiti border, but it was spotted and shattered by US artillery fire. The weather was overcast and wet, with poor visibility of only about 1,500m. The 2nd Armored Brigade of the RGFC Medina Armored Division was deployed in a reverse-slope defense, but the site was poorly chosen. The US 2nd Brigade, 1st Armored Division approached the Iraqi defenses shortly after noon on February 27. The Iraqis were unaware of their approach, lacking a proper security zone and unable to see the Abrams due to the weather. The ensuing firefight was extremely one-sided. The thermal sights on the M1A1 tanks allowed the American crews to accurately locate and target the Iraqi armored vehicles, while the Iraqi armored vehicles were hampered by the poor weather and mediocre tank optics. Within 15 minutes of the start of the tank duel, 37 Iraqi armored vehicles had been set on fire, many T-72 tanks exploding in a gruesome fireball with the turrets tumbling through the air. In less than an hour of fighting on the "Medina Ridge," the 2nd "Iron" Brigade had knocked out 59 T-72 tanks, 29 BMP-1, six Strela-10 air defense missile vehicles, and four other armored vehicles.

US Army soldiers inspect an entrenched BMP-1 infantry fighting vehicle of the RGFC Medina Division days after the fighting with VII Corps.

Endgame, February 27–March 2, 1991

The neighboring 1st Brigade, 1st Armored Division faced the Medina's 14th Mechanized Brigade and elements of the 46th Mechanized Brigade of the 12th Armored Division. The US Army attack began at a range of 4,000m using thermal sights, while the Iraqis were in the process of rearming and re-fueling their vehicles. The Iraqi units were unprepared for the attack and generally oriented towards the south instead of facing the west where the attack emanated. The 1st Armored Division's 3rd Brigade was the last to crest the ridge around 1300hrs and encountered the 2nd Mechanized Brigade of the RGFC Medina Division, which it methodically destroyed with long-range gunfire from the M1A1 tanks and TOW missile fire from the Bradleys. By the end of February 27, the 1st Armored Division had destroyed the Medina Division, knocking out 186 tanks and 127 armored infantry vehicles.[2]

The southern-most of the VII Corps heavy maneuver divisions was the British 1st Armoured Division. The division's mission was to shield the right flank of the advancing VII Corps and to destroy the Iraqi 7 Corps. During the night of February 26, the Challenger tanks and Warrior infantry vehicles chewed through two armored and one infantry battalion of the 52nd Armored Division on the approaches to the Wadi al-Batin. By February 27, the collapse of the Iraqi Army was evident to the British commanders and the pursuit phase of the operation began. One important issue was the boundaries on either side, since the UK 1st Armoured Division was wedged between the Egyptian 2 Corps on the right flank to the south and the US Army 1st Infantry Division on the left flank to the north. The problem of friendly fire was a recurring worry due to the usual battlefield confusion compounded by the awful weather conditions. At 0915hrs, A Squadron of the Queen's Dragoon Guards crossed the Wadi al-Batin into Kuwait. The final mission in Kuwait was in a state of flux until the last minute. VII Corps for a time suggested that the division would wheel right along the eastern side of Wadi al-Batin to clear a logistics corridor. This scheme was eventually discarded, and the division was tasked with a push immediately to the east towards Objective Cobalt to secure the highway to Basra, roughly 20 miles (30km) northwest of Kuwait City. This put the division on the northern flank of the US 2nd Marine Division, and the southern flank of the US 1st Infantry Division. In the absence of any sizeable Iraqi resistance, a final cavalry advance was ordered, spearheaded by the 7th Brigade, since a ceasefire was expected shortly.

Iraqi combat losses in VII Corps sector

Unit	Tanks	APC/IFV	Artillery	Air defense	Trucks
1st ID	382	235	82	33	206
1st AD	341	294	64	32	504
1 (UK) AD	139	109	30	5	53
3rd AD	203	306	45	8	241
1st Cav	34	14	44	10	75
2nd ACR	161	180	12	6	81
11th AB	90	86	8	11	69
Total	**1,350**	**1,224**	**285**	**105**	**1,229**

2   For more details on the Battle of the Medina Ridge, see: Steven Zaloga, *M1 Abrams vs T-72 Ural: Operation* Desert Storm *1991*, Osprey Duel 18 (2009).

Jubilation as Saudi and Kuwaiti units of JFC-East liberate Kuwait City on February 26, 1991.

THE LIBERATION OF KUWAIT CITY

The liberation of Kuwait City had political implications, and an agreement had been reached before the war that the JFC would be given the honor. After the Marines had captured Kuwait International Airport on February 27, the I MEF halted movement towards the city to permit the JFC to move its forces forward. The JFC commander, Lt. Gen. Khalid, had instructed both JFC-East to make up a task force with troops for all six Gulf Cooperation Council countries, while at the same time instructed JFC-North to prepare a similar task force from Egypt, Syria, Kuwait, and Saudi Arabia. Kuwaiti resistance fighters had taken over much of the city in the wake of the Iraqi retreat, and the arrival of the JFC task forces was greeted with considerable popular jubilation. Nevertheless, the situation in the city was chaotic and on February 28, Shaikh Said, the Kuwaiti Crown Prince, ordered a state of emergency to be imposed and for Kuwaiti troops to take control of the city.

ENDGAME

By G+4, February 27, the fighting appeared to be nearing its conclusion. That afternoon, British Foreign Minister Douglas Hurd visited the White House in Washington DC to discuss immediate plans. There was little willingness to negotiate with Saddam, and both the British and American sides favored an imposed, unilateral ceasefire. Concerns were voiced over major issues such as the return of Coalition prisoners-of-war as an immediate and non-negotiable demand, including the roughly 25,000 Kuwaiti citizens still in Iraqi hands.

President Bush convened a meeting that afternoon. Other senior leaders favored a ceasefire as soon as possible, to some extent to counter the public perception that the Coalition was needlessly butchering the Iraqis based on sensational television accounts about the "Highway of Death." Gen. Colin

The Iraqi Army ignited additional oil field fires during their retreat, creating a hellish landscape in some parts of Kuwait.

Powell suggested that the ceasefire decision at this point was political and not military, in view of the level of destruction suffered by the Iraqi armed forces.

On the night of February 27, Powell called Schwarzkopf at CENTCOM and warned him that President Bush was planning to impose a ceasefire by 0500hrs (Gulf time). The senior US Army commander, Lt. Gen. Yeosock of Third Army, was informed of these plans and began to contact the corps commanders to determine whether their forces could be disengaged from the fighting by that time. Both XVIII Corps and VII Corps had expected to spend another day wrapping up the final destruction of the Republican Guard and were surprised at the sudden decision to call a halt to the fighting. Nevertheless, they began issuing instructions to their units to begin to take up a defensive posture and halt active military operations by 0500hrs on February 28. The timing was later delayed to 0800hrs. Reports that large numbers of RGFC T-72 tanks were fleeing over the Euphrates bridges led to instructions around 0400hrs to resume attacks to secure as many bridges and road junctions as possible to limit Iraqi withdrawals.

The Iraqi Army was confused about the ceasefire, and senior commanders in Baghdad were still unaware of the extent of XVIII Airborne Corps' and VII Corps' advance into southeast Iraq. Baghdad continued to order RGFC units to escape out of the Basra pocket into central Iraq. A more immediate concern was the sudden outbreak of ethnic insurgencies. The long-abused Shiites in southern Iraq and the Kurds along the Turkish border began taking over towns in their regions and fighting with Iraqi police and military units.

One of the main routes out of the Basra pocket was the Hammar Causeway over the Hawr al-Hammar marshes. In particular, Baghdad

A pair of Iraqi T-55 tanks of the 1st Tank Regiment, 26th Armored Brigade, 5th Mechanized Division lie abandoned on the Basra–Kuwait City Highway near Kuwait City on February 26, 1991, after their capture by the I MEF. This Iraqi division fought at Khafji and took part in the February 26–27 counter-attack against the I MEF.

ordered the largely intact Hammurabi Division to escape. Some Iraqi troops blundered into outposts of the US 24th Infantry Division on March 1, but the main troubles erupted in the pre-dawn hours of March 2, when the JSTARS surveillance aircraft spotted an enormous column of vehicles heading for the Hammar Causeway. This was the 17th Brigade of the RGFC Hammurabi Division. Around 0800hrs, an Iraqi soldier fired an RPG-7 antitank rocket at a Bradley sitting at one of the outposts, and a column of Iraqi tanks and vehicles began firing at the American outpost.

The final fighting of the war occurred on March 2, 1991, when a brigade of the RGFC Hammurabi Division attempted to escape the Basra pocket and made the mistake of engaging the 24th Infantry Division outside the Rumaylah oil fields. Here one of the division's M1A1 Abrams tanks moves forward towards the fighting.

APACHE ATTACK, BATTLE OF RUMAYLAH, MARCH 2, 1991 (PP. 84–85)

On March 2, 1991, the 17th Brigade, Hammurabi RGFC Division attempted to escape out of the Basra pocket via the Hammar Causeway over the Hawr al-Hammar marshes near Rumaylah. After several skirmishes on the ground, the US Army's 24th Infantry Division (Mech) ordered the AH-64A Apache attack helicopters **(1)** of the 1st Battalion, 24th Aviation Brigade to destroy the Hammurabi columns. The Apaches began the attack by destroying the vehicles at both ends of the column, trapping the remaining vehicles between. The battalion subsequently targeted all air defense threats, especially the ZSU-23-4 Shilka vehicles that were armed with radar-directed quad 23mm automatic cannons. With the air defense threat defeated, the battalion then set about systematically attacking the trapped column. They fired a total of 107 Hellfire missiles **(2)**, scoring 102 hits, and also fired all of their 70mm Hydra high-explosive rockets **(3)**. The 17th Brigade was largely destroyed, including 30 T-72 tanks **(4)**, 187 AFVs, 34 artillery pieces, and 400 trucks and other vehicles.

The 24th Infantry Division was itching for a fight and determined to show the Iraqis that no combat incidents would be tolerated. The 24th's divisional artillery initiated a barrage of cluster munitions and artillery-scattered mines on either side of the causeway. This was followed by an attack by the division's Apache battalion that sealed off the causeway at either end and then systematically destroyed the Hammurabi column on the bridge using Hellfires, 70mm Hydra rockets, and 30mm autocannon fire. Other elements of the 24th Infantry Division destroyed Iraqi vehicles milling around the approaches to the causeway. At the end of this one-sided fight, the 17th Brigade had been largely destroyed, including 30 T-72 tanks, 187 AFVs, 34 artillery pieces, and 400 trucks and other vehicles. US losses consisted of a single Abrams tank that burned out when it was set on fire by a massive explosion from a nearby explosives-laden Iraqi truck. Iraqi troop losses were much smaller than equipment losses, since once the column was trapped on the causeway, the Iraqi troops fled their vehicles and escaped through the marshes. This was the last major ground combat of the 100-Hour War.

Another skirmish was narrowly avoided on the morning of March 2. CENTCOM had announced that truce negotiations to end the war would be conducted at the airport at Safwan on March 3 on the misunderstanding that it was already in American hands. This was not the case, and it was in fact occupied by a sizeable Iraqi force of about five battalions. A column from the 1st Infantry Division was sent to the site in the early morning to occupy it. The Iraqis refused to budge, so the US Air Force sent a flight of

A burning T-72M1 tank of the RGFC Hammurabi Division following its encounter with the 24th Infantry Division (Mech) on March 2, 1991.

Troops from Saudi Arabia, Syria, Oman, and other Coalition armies gather for review by King Fahd of Saudi Arabia as they take part in an assembly on March 8, 1991 celebrating the end of the war.

A-10 aircraft over the airfield. The US task force warned the Iraqis that the A-10s would attack on their next pass. As a result, the Iraqis withdrew from the airfield by noon.

The negotiations at Safwan on March 3 were hasty and controversial. Schwarzkopf and Khalid led the Coalition delegation. The meeting was held so soon after the ceasefire that Washington had not had the time to dispatch a senior civilian diplomat to accompany him, and he received no formal instructions. Schwarzkopf's main aims were to terminate the conflict and retrieve prisoners-of-war. There were no plans to march on Baghdad and this was not used as a diplomatic lever to extract concessions from the Iraqis. Nor was there any explicit effort made to overthrow Saddam, although many senior leaders expected this to occur due to the disastrous conduct of the war.

Lt. Gen. Sultan Ahmed Hashim, the army chief of staff, led the Iraqi delegation. The Iraqis were forced to accept the Coalition demands. The one concession requested by the Iraqi delegation was permission to fly helicopters in southeastern Iraq so long as they did not overfly Coalition positions. The Iraqi delegation justified the need to use helicopters for government use due to the damage done to civilian infrastructure. Schwarzkopf conceded this point, thinking it was harmless. It later transpired that the Iraqi delegation wished to use helicopters to suppress rebellions that had broken out throughout southern Iraq. By the end of the day, the truce ending the war had been signed.

For the Iraqi Army, the end of the war against the Coalition was only a momentary respite from fighting. The rebellions against the Baathist regime quickly overwhelmed the country. The initial outbreaks involved Shiites and disgruntled soldiers in the Basra area, followed by many cities in the south including Najaf, Amarah, Diwaniya, Hilla, Karbala,

Kut, Nasiriyah, and Samawah. Radio stations sponsored by the CIA had encouraged rebellion, as did other radio stations based in Saudi Arabia. It is by no means clear that these inspired the rebellion given the magnitude and spontaneity of the uprisings. The troubles soon spread to the Kurdish areas in the north. The rebellion lasted more than a month and was brutally suppressed by the Republican Guard. There are no accurate figures for the scale of the civilian losses, but some sources cite 100,000 dead; millions of civilians were displaced, with many fleeing into neighboring Turkey. Regime losses in the army, Republican Guard and police, are believed to have exceeded the combat casualties of the Gulf War. Saddam himself later admitted that, "The traitorous rebellion was more difficult than the [war] before it."

On March 10, 1991, US forces began withdrawing from Kuwait and back into Saudi Arabia as the first step towards withdrawal from the region, bringing an end to Operation *Desert Storm*. On April 11, 1991, the UN Security Council agreed that Iraq's acceptance of the ceasefire agreement had satisfied earlier UN requirements, formally concluding the 1991 Gulf War.

Gen. Norman Schwarzkopf, CENTCOM commander-in-chief, next to Lt. Gen. Khalid bin Sultan al-Saud, dictates conditions for a ceasefire during the negotiations at Safwan on March 3, 1991 to the Iraqi delegation. The Iraqi general with his face turned to the camera is Lt. Gen. Sultan Ahmed Hashim al-Tai, Iraqi Army chief of staff.

THE CAMPAIGN IN RETROSPECT

The 1991 Gulf War was one of the most rapid and decisive military defeats of the twentieth century. Operation *Desert Storm* demonstrated that air power was still unable to win wars by itself, but that it was the decisive force to attain victory while enduring a minimum of friendly casualties. The Iraqi Army collapsed barely a day after the start of the ground campaign due to the demoralization and casualties endured from a month of bombardment. The disparity in casualties between Iraq and the Coalition illustrates this contrast. Iraqi soldiers killed in action were estimated to be about 10,000; there were a further 82,000 prisoners-of-war. Coalition casualties were 347 killed, of which 181 were due to enemy action, 44 to friendly fire, and the remainder to accidents and other causes. The extent of damage inflicted on the Iraqi Army is evident in the chart below depicting the Iraqi armed forces before and after the war.

Iraqi military strength before and after *Desert Storm*

	January 1991	Postwar
Tanks	5,700	2,300
APC/IFV	5,100	2,700
Artillery	3,800	1,800
Divisions	67	27
Combat aircraft	750	340

Source: "Iraqi Military Capabilities through 1999: NIE 94–19," CIA Director of Central Intelligence, July 1994

Despite the magnitude of the Iraqi defeat, there were numerous controversies swirling around the conduct of the war. Many US Army commanders felt that the war had been terminated a day or two too soon. A major goal of the war had been the destruction of the Republican Guard. However, a large fraction of the Republican Guard divisions managed to escape to Basra due to the ceasefire. On March 1, US overhead imagery showed that 842 tanks and 1,412 other AFVs had escaped. Of these, 365 T-72 tanks were assessed to belong to the RGFC, amounting to about half of their prewar strength of 786. The goal of destroying the RGFC had failed due to the early ceasefire. Furthermore, the RGFC formed the backbone of the Iraqi forces that suppressed the revolt that followed the defeat.

Schwarzkopf blamed the VII Corps commander, Lt. Gen. Franks, for being too slow and methodical. Yet the VII Corps had conducted the campaign more swiftly than envisioned in the original plans. The main source of the premature conclusion of the fighting was Washington DC, where national leaders were concerned that a repeat of the "Highway of Death" on the Basra highway would sour the American public on the war.

The war left Saddam in power. The war aims did not explicitly intend to dethrone Saddam and the Baathist regime, though many expected that the magnitude of the defeat inevitably would do so. Saddam's continued leadership created lingering problems in the region. In 1994, there was another war scare when the Iraqi Army appeared ready to invade Kuwait again. Although the UN obliged Iraq to end its chemical weapons and missile programs, and destroy their stocks of these weapons, there remained concerns that Saddam was undertaking a surreptitious program. This was one of the causes of a renewed war in 2003. Since the 1991 war had failed to oust Saddam, a principal mission of the 2003 war was to capture Saddam and oust the Baathists from power. This was accomplished, but Iraq fell into a decade of insurgency and violence. The chaos and violence following the 2003 war cast a dark shadow over the legacy of the 1991 conflict, leading it to be dubbed a "triumph without victory."

THE BATTLEFIELD TODAY

A T-62 tank serving as a monument to Operation *Desert Storm* outside the Area Support Group – Kuwait headquarters at Camp Arifjan, Kuwait in 2023. (US DoD/ASG-K by 1st Lt. Austin May)

The battlefields of the 1991 Gulf War have not been memorialized. In large measure, this is due to their locations in remote desert areas that discourage casual tourism. The most extensive memorialization of the war comes in the form of numerous Iraqi weapons, especially tanks and armored vehicles, which were brought back to army bases and military museums of the victorious armies. Most army posts in the United States have an Iraqi tank or two on display, and the British Tank Museum at Bovington and French museum at Saumur have numerous Iraqi trophies.

FURTHER READING

BOOKS AND ARTICLES

Ali Altobchi, *Al-Hussein: Iraqi Indigenous Conventional Arms Programs 1980–2003*, Helion: Warwick (2003)

Hazim Abd al-Razzaq al-Ayyubi, "Forty-Three Missiles on the Zionist Entity," (nine parts) *Amman al-Arab al-Yamn*, November 1998; Translation by FBIS: Reston, VA (1998)

Stephen Bourque, *Jayhawk! The VII Corps in the Persian Gulf War*, US Army Chief of Military History: Washington DC (2001)

Tom Carhart, *Iron Soldiers: How America's 1st Armored Division Crushed Iraq's Elite Republican Guard*, Pocket: New York (1994)

James Cooke, *100 Miles from Baghdad: With the French in Desert Storm*, Praeger: New York (1993)

Charles Cureton, *With the 1st Marine Division in Desert Shield and Desert Storm*, USMC History Division: Quantico (1993)

Sir Peter de la Billière, *Storm Command: A Personal Account of the Gulf War*, HarperCollins: London (1992)

Thomas Dinackus, *Order of Battle: Allied Ground Forces of Operation Desert Storm*, Hellgate: Central Point (2000)

Gregory Fontenot, *The 1st Infantry Division and the US Army Transformed: Road to Victory in Desert Storm 1970–1991*, University of Missouri: Colombia (2017)

Michael Gordon, Bernard Trainor, *The Generals' War: The Inside Story of the Conflict in the Gulf*, Little, Brown: New York (1995)

Pesach Malovany, *Wars of Modern Babylon: A History of the Iraqi Army from 1921 to 2003*, University Press of Kentucky: Lexington (2017)

Douglas Macgregor, *Warrior's Rage: The Great Tank Battle of 73 Easting*, Naval Institute: Annapolis (2009)

G. J. Michaels, *Tip of the Spear: US Marine Light Armor in the Gulf War*, Naval Institute: Annapolis (1998)

David Morris, *Storm on the Horizon: Khafji – The Battle that Changed the Course of the Gulf War*, Ballentine: New York (2005)

Dennis Mroczkowski, *With the 2nd Marine Division in Desert Shield and Desert Storm*, USMC History Division: Quantico (1993)

Nigel Pearce, *The Shield and the Sabre: The Desert Rats in the Gulf 1990–1991*, HMSO (1992)

David Pierson, *Tuskers: An Armor Battalion in the Gulf War*, Darlington: Darlington (1997)

Robert Scales Jr., *Certain Victory: US Army in the Gulf War*, US Army Chief of Staff (1993)

Frank Schubert, et al., *The Whirlwind War*, US Center of Military History: Washington DC (1995)

HRH Khaled bin Sultan, *Desert Warrior: A Personal View of the Gulf War by the Joint Forces Commander*, HarperCollins: New York (1995)

Martin Stanton, "The Saudi Arabian National Guard Motorized Brigades," *Armor*, March–April 1996, pp. 6–11

Richard Swain, *Lucky War: Third Army in Desert Storm*, US Army Command and General Staff College (1994)

Thomas Tailor, *Lightning in the Storm: The 101st Air Assault Division in the Gulf War*, Hippocrene: New York (1995)

Charles Toomey, *XVIII Airborne Corps in* Desert Storm, Hellgate: Central Pont (2004)

Paul Westermeyer, *Liberating Kuwait: US Marines in the Gulf War 1990–1991*, USMC History Division: Quantico (2008)

Paul Westermeyer, *Al-Khafji 28 January–1 February 1991: US Marines in the Gulf War 1990–1991*, USMC History Division: Quantico (2008)

Kevin Woods, *The Mother of All Battles: Saddam Hussein's Strategic Plan for the Persian Gulf War*, Naval Institute Press: Annapolis (2014)

Kevin Woods, *Um Al-Ma'arik (The Mother of All Battles): Operational and Strategic Insights from an Iraqi Perspective*, IDA: Alexandria, VA (2008)

Kevin Woods, et al., *Saddam's Generals: Perspectives of the Iran–Iraq War*, IDA: Alexandria (2011)

Kevin Woods, et al., *Saddam's War: An Iraqi Military Perspective of the Iran–Iraq War*, National Defense University: Washington DC (2009)

Kevin Woods, et al., *A View of Operation* Iraqi Freedom *from Saddam's Senior Leadership*, US Joint Forces Command: Norfolk (2006)

GOVERNMENT REPORTS

3rd Armored Division – Operation Desert Storm, 3rd Armored Division (1992)

73 Easting: Lessons Learned from Desert Storm, DARPA/IDA: Alexandria (April 1992)

Armor/Anti-Armor Operations in Southwest Asia, US Marine Corps Research Center: Quantico (1992)

Conduct of the Persian Gulf War: Final Report to Congress, US Department of Defense (1992)

Desert Shield *and* Desert Storm*: Emerging Observations*, US Army Armor Center: Ft. Knox (1994)

The Iraqi Army: Organization and Tactics: Handbook 100-91, US National Training Center (January 1991)

Operation Desert Shield/Desert Storm *Executive Summary*, US CENTCOM (July 11, 1991)

Operation Desert Storm, *The Military Intelligence Story: A view from the G-2 Third US Army*, Third US Army (April 1991)

US Space Command – Operations Desert Shield *and* Desert Storm *Assessment*, HQ AFSPACECOM (January 1992)

INDEX

Figures in **bold** refer to illustrations.

AAVP-7A1 (Assault Amphibian Vehicle) (US) 24, **58**, **60**, **61**, 62
AFVs (armored fighting vehicles) 43, 51, 57, 61, 63, 70, **86**, 87
   MT-LB armored transporter (Iraq) 72, **73**, 74
aircraft 19, 30, **39**, 51, **90**
   A-6 Intruder (US) 72
   A-10 (US) 34, 42–43, **43**, 45, 51, 75, **88**
   B-52 (US) 42, **42**
   F-16 (US) 75
   F-111 (US) 34, 42, **42**
   Mirage F-1 (Iraq) 44
   RC-135 Rivet Joint (US) 29
   Tornado F3 (UK) 37
APCs (armored personnel carriers) 28, 43, 51, 78, **90**
   Cadillac-Gage-V-150 (US) **27**, 54–55, **56**, 57, **57**
   M113 (US) 22, 28, 63
   VAB (Véhicule de l'Avant Blindé) (France) 27
   YW-531 (Iraq) 16, **16**
Appliqué Armor 24, **24**, 60
Arab Coalition forces 26–29, **27**, **28**, **88**
   Egyptian 28, **28**, 33, 36, **62**, 63, 80
   Qatari 57
   Syrian 28
artillery 16–17, 22–23, 28, **62**
as-Salman town and airbase 64–66, **67**, 68

Baath Party 8, 11, 39, 91
Battle for Ras al-Khafji 5, 6, 50–58, **52–53**, **54–55**, **56**, **57**, 63, 83
Battle of 73 Easting 7, 74, **76–77**
Battle of Burqan 63
Battle of Medina Ridge 7, **7**, 80
Battle of the Hammar Causeway (Rumaylah) 7, **83**, 83–87, **84–85**, **86**, 87
BFME (British Forces Middle East) 10, 45
   1st Armoured Division 5, 10, 21, **25**, 25, 26, 36, 69, 70, **70**, 78, 80
   4th Armoured Brigade 25
   7th Armoured Brigade **25**, 25
   regiments 25–26, **26**
      Queen's Dragoon Guards 80
      Royal Scots Dragoon Guards **69**, 70
Boomer, Lt. Gen. Walter 10, 35
"Budd lights" 67
Bull, Gerald 16, **17**
Bush, George H. W. 4, 6, 9, 34, 35, 36, 81, 82

CAS missions 51, 72
ceasefire and truce talks 9, 81–82, 87, 88, 89, **89**
CENTCOM (US Central Command) 4, 9, 10, 20, 21, 29, 34, **34**, 82, 87, 88, **89**

CFVs (Cavalry Fighting Vehicles)
   M3 Bradley (US) 21, 22, 68, 74, 75
Cheney, Dick 9, **9**, 34, **34**, 35
Cold War 4

de la Billière, Lt. Gen. Sir Peter 10
deaths 39, 43, 49, 50, 57, 62, 89, 90
desertion 43, **44**, 61

E-3B AWACS (Airborne Warning and Control System) (US) 29
EE-9 Cascavel armored car (Iraq) **15**
ethnic insurgencies 82, 88–89

Fahd, King 10, **88**
FOBs (forward operating bases) 66–67
Franks, Gen. Frederick M. 43, 90
French Army
   Division Daguet 26, 36, 64, 67, 68
friendly fire **28**, 67, 80, 90

GCC (Gulf Cooperation Council) 4
GMID (General Military Intelligence Directorate) 19, 39, 40
GPS navigation 30, 67, 74

helicopters 18, 23, 25, 49, **54–55**, **56**, 67
   AC-130 gunship (US) 51, 75
   AH-1 Cobra (US) **24**, 25, 51, 63, 66, 68, 75
   AH-64 Apache (US) 23, **23**, 41, 66, 74, **84–85**, **86**, 87
   CH-47 Chinook (US) **37**, 49, 66
   UH-60 Black Hawk (US) 23, **23**, 66, 67
"Highway of Death" 71, 72, **72**, 81, **83**, 91
Hussein, Saddam 4, 5, 7, 8, 8–9, 18, 19, 32, 33, 39, 40, 41, 44, 50, 71, 81, 88, 89, 91

identification markings **28**
IFVs (Infantry Fighting Vehicles) 28, **90**
   BMP-1 (Iraq) 13, 14, **14**, 16, 43, 68, 74, 75, 78, **78**
   BMP-2 (Iraq) 28
   M2 Bradley (US) 22, 25, 26, 66, 67, 69, 80, 83
   Warrior (UK) **26**, 26, 70, 80
intelligence 4, 19, 29–30, 63
international Coalition 4, 5, 19–20, **20**
IPSA pipeline 74
Iran–Iraq War 4, 8, 11, 14, 15, **15**, 17, 18, 20, 50
Iranian hostage crisis (1979) 20
Iraqi Air Force 5, 6, 44
Iraqi arms imports 14, **14–15**, **16**, **17**
Iraqi Army 5, 6, 8, 11–13, **12**, 14, 16, 17, 30, 32, 36, 40, 41, 58, 69, 70, 82, 88, 90, **90**
   brigades 43, 51, 61, 73, 74, 78, 80
   9th RGFC 74, 75
   14th Mechanized 80

   15th Mechanized 51, 63
   17th 83, 84–85, 86
   22nd 61, 63
   29th RGFC Mechanized 75
   46th Mechanized 80
   Brigade 223 19, 44
   Brigade 226 50
   Missile Brigade 224 44, 45, 46–47, **48**, 49
   Missile Brigade 225 50, **50**
   RGFC Special Forces 37
   corps
      2 Corps 32, 36, 71
      3 Corps 32–33, 50–51, 60, 64, 71, 72
      4 Corps 33, 50, 63, 71
      7 Corps 13, 33, 71, 80
      Jihad 13, 71, 73, 78
   divisions 37, 43
      1st "Abu Ubayda ibn al-Jarrah" Mechanized 18, 51
      3rd "Saladin" Armored 13, 51, 63, 64, 72
      5th Mechanized 51, 57, 61, 63, 83
      7th 63
      8th Infantry 63, 64
      10th "Nasr ibn Sayyar" Armored 13, 15, 73
      12th Armored 13, 43, 73, 80
      18th 63
      26th Infantry 68, 69, 70
      27th Infantry 15
      29th Infantry 61
      45th Infantry 64, 67
      47th Infantry 68
      48th Infantry 17, 69
      49th Infantry 68
      51st Mechanized 13
      52nd Armored 13, 15, 43, 80
      Hammurabi RGFC Armored 37, 39, 73, **83**, 83, 84–85, **86**, 87, **87**
      Medina RGFC Armored 37, 39, 73, 75, 78, **78**, 80
      RGFC Adnan Mechanized 78
      Tawakalna RGFC Mechanized 73, 74, 75, **75**
   People's Army 11
   RGFC (Republican Guard Forces Command) 4, 5, 6, 7, 8, 9, 14, **14**, 16, 17, 32, 33, 35, 36, 37, 40, 50, 68, 71, 73, 76–77, 78, 82, 89, 90
Iraqi Navy
   Brigade 440 51, **52–53**
Iraqi strategy and aims 4, 8–9, 14, 32–34, 39–40, 41, 44, 46–47, **48**, 49, 50, 50–57, **54–55**, **56**, 58, 63–64, 75, 78, 83–87
   and withdrawal 71, 71–72, 73, **82**, 82–83, 88
Israeli strategy and actions 44
   missile attacks on 46–47, **48**, 50

JCS (Joint Chiefs of Staff) 35
JDOP (Joint Directorate of Planning) 34

95

JFC (Joint Forces Command) 10, 36, 51, **59**, 60, **62**, **63**, 70, 81, **81**
JIC (Joint Intelligence Center) 29
JSOC (Joint Special Operations Command) 45

KARI air defense system 41
kill claims 42, **42**, 45, 49
Kuwait
  invasion of 4, 5, 6, 8–9, 11, 18, 37–39, 38
  liberation of 81, 81
Kuwaiti Army 28, **28**, 37, 39

LAVs (light armored vehicles) 25, 51, **64**
logistics and supplies 21, 41

M9 ACE (armored combat earthmover) (US) **58**, 61, 62
M728 CEV (combat engineer vehicle) (US) **66**
MARCENT 10, 35, 36
matèriel losses 42, **42**, 43, 49, 51, 57, 61, 63, 70, 73, 74, 75, 78, 80, **80**, 84–85, **86**, 87
memorials and monuments 92, **92**
military satellites 30, 45
military strengths and complements 11–13, 14, **14–15**, 15, **20**, 21, 23, 24, 25–26, **40**, **42**, 43, **44**, 67, 78, **90**
minefields 33, **60**, 75
missile launchers 45
  9P113 (Iraq) 50
  M901 (US) 44, 45
  al-Waleed (Iraq) 18, 19
morale 41, 43, 90
munitions drops **42**

NRO (National Reconnaissance Office) 29

oil field fires **82**
operations 25, 26, 35
  Daguet 10, 26
  Desert Shield (August 1990–January 1991) 6, 21, 39
  Desert Storm (January–February 1991) 9, 89, 90
  Granby 10, 25
orders of battle **31**

Pakistani forces 28
Powell, Gen. Colin 9, 9–10, 20, 34, **34**, 35, 81–82
POWs 42, 61, 63, 64, 69, 73, 81, 88

radar systems 17, 19, 23, 41, **42**, 45
  APY-7 (US) 29, 30
  JSTARS (US) 29, 30, 51, 72, 73, 83
RAF **37**, 49
ranges 18, 23, **49**, 74, 80
reconnaissance **23**, 26
Roquejeoffre, Général d'armée Michel 10
Royal Navy 51

RSLF (Royal Saudi Land Forces) 26, 27–28, 36, **49**, **62**, **63**, **88**
  8th MODA Brigade 51
Rumaylah oil fields 75, **83**

"Saddam Line" 33, **40**, **58**, 62
Safwan airport 87–88
Said, Shaikh 81
SANG (Saudi Arabia National Guard) 6, 27, 34, **52–53**, 57
  2nd King Abdulaziz Brigade 51, **54–55**, 56, **57**, 57
  7th Combined Arms Battalion **54–55**, 56, 57
SAS (Special Air Service) 10, 45, 49
Saud, Prince Lt. Gen. Khalid bin Sultan al- 10, **10**, 51, 88, **89**
Saudi interests and aims 4, 10, 21, 34, 35, 51, **52–53**, **54–55**, 56
Schwarzkopf, Gen. Norman, Jr. 9, **9**, 20, 29, **34**, **34**, 35, 36, 82, **88**, **89**, 90
Scimitar CVR-T (Combat Vehicle Reconnaissance) (UK) 26
Scorpion CVR-T (UK) 26
Second Gulf War (2003) 91

Tai, Lt. Gen. Sultan Ahmed Hashim al- 9, 88, **89**
"tank plinking" 42
tank versus tank battles (February 26–27, 1991) 73–74, **76–77**, 83
tanks 15, 23, 27, 28, 39, 57, 61, 63, 78
  9P122 tank destroyer (Iraq) **69**
  AMX-30 (France and Qatar) 26, 27, **27**, 51, **56**, 57, 64, **68**
  Challenger 1 Mk 3 (UK) 25, **25**, **70**, 80
  M1A1 Abrams (US) 21–22, **22**, 24, 62, **66**, 67, 68, **69**, 70, 74, 75, 78, 80
  M60A1 (US) 24, **24**, 27, 51, **60**, 62
  T-55 (Iraq) 15, 43, 57, 64, 68, 73, 74, **83**
  T-62 (Iraq) **72**, **92**
  T-72 (Iraq) 13, 14, 15–16, 22, 39, **66**, 74, 75, **75**, 78, 82, **84–85**, **86**, 87, **87**, 90
  Type 69-II (Iraq) **67**, **70**
Tariq Project 40
terrain factors 36, 67, 73
thermal imaging 22, 74, 75, 78, 80
trade sanctions 6, 34
training 20, **23**, **24**, **25**, **27**, 45, 75

UN Security Council 4, 7, 39, 89, 91
  Resolution 678 35, 36
uniforms **20**
US Air Force 34, **43**, 49, 51, 87–88
US Army 17, 20, 49, 78
  ADA (Air Defense Artillery) 44, 45
  brigades 64, 67, 75, 78, 80
  corps 21
    VII 5, 6, 22, 25, 35, 36, 40, 43, 58, 65, 68, 69, 69, 73–74, 78, 78, 82, 90
    XVIII Airborne 5, 35, 36, 40, 64–66, 65, 67, 68, 82

Delta Force 45, 49
divisions
  1st Armored 22, 68, 70, 78, 80
  1st Cavalry 58, 70, 78
  1st Infantry 69, 70, 74, 78, 80, 87
  2nd Armored 61
  3rd Armored 68, 69, 70, 74, 75, 78
  24th Infantry 17, 21, 66, 67, 83, 83–87, **84–85**, **86**, 87
  82nd Airborne 6, 21, 23, 64, 66
  101st Airborne 20, 21, 23, 66, 67
regiments 20, 21, 67
  2nd Armored Cavalry 68, **70**, 73, 74, 75, 78
  4th Cavalry 67, 68
Third Army 10, 21, 82
US/Coalition strategy 9, 34–36, **39**, 41, 42, 45–49, 51, 82, 89, 90–91
  air campaign 41, 42, **42**, 43, 44, 45
  ground campaign 58, 58–70, 59, 60, 61, 62, 65, 69, 70, 72–78, 79, 80, 83–88
  "Great Wheel" maneuver 69, 70, 76–77
US Marine Corps 21, 24, 35–36, 51, 56, 58, 61, 63, **64**, 72
  1st Marine Division 40, 60, 61, 63, 64, 72
  1st 'Tiger' Brigade 61, 72–73
  2nd Marine Division 58, 60, 61, 62, 64, 72, 80
  I MEF (Marine Expeditionary Force) 5, 7, 23, 35, 36, 60, 61, 61, 63, 71, 72, 73, 81, 83
  MPF (Maritime Prepositioning Force) 21
US Navy 51, **62**, 63
Navy SEALs 51
US Security Council 4, 6, 36

Wadi al-Batin **70**, 71
weaponry 8, **16**, 16, 17, **17**, 22, 24, 26, **27**, **42**, 51, **60**, **62**, 72
  90mm Cockerill gun (Saudi Arabia) **54–55**, 56, 57
  chemical weapons 33–34, 60, 91
  Hellfire missile (US) **84–85**, **86**, 87
  Hydra rocket (US) **84–85**, **86**, 87
  Luna-M/FROG-7 rocket (Iraq) 6, 19, 50, 50
  M109 155mm self-propelled gun (US) 16, 17, 22–23, 28, 62
  M270 Multiple Rocket Launcher (US) 22, 23
  Patriot missile (US) 44, 45, 49, 49
  RPG-7 rocket (Iraq) 67, 83
  Scud missile (Iraq) 5, 6, 18, 44, 45
    al-Husayn missile 18, 18, 44, 46–47, 48, 49, 49, 50
  WMD (weapons-of-mass-destruction) 41
  ZSU-23-4 Shilka self-propelled gun (Iraq) 17, 18, 86
weather conditions 59–60, 66, 67, 68, 74, 78, 80

Yeosock, Lt. Gen. John 10, 82